Essays *from* Essex

Essays
from
Essex

SYDNEY M. WILLIAMS

Illustrations by Alexander C. Williams

BAUHAN PUBLISHING
PETERBOROUGH . NEW HAMPSHIRE
2023

Library of Congress Cataloging-in-Publication Data
Names: Williams, Sydney M. (Sydney Messer), 1941- author. | Williams, Alexander C., illustrator.
Title: Essays from Essex / Sydney M. Williams ; illustrations by Alexander C. Williams.
Description: Peterborough, New Hampshire : Bauhan Publishing, 2022. | Includes bibliographical references. |
Identifiers: LCCN 2022009728 (print) | LCCN 2022009729 (ebook) | ISBN 9780872333482 (trade paperback) | ISBN 9780872333499 (ebook)
Subjects: LCSH: Williams, Sydney M. (Sydney Messer), 1941- | Williams, Sydney M. (Sydney Messer), 1941—Family. | Families—Connecticut—Essex. | Nature. | Essex (Conn—Biography. | Essex (Conn—Environmental conditions.
Classification: LCC F104.E8 W55 2023 (print) | LCC F104.E8 (ebook) | DDC 974.6/6—dc23/eng/20220310
LC record available at https://lccn.loc.gov/2022009728
LC ebook record available at https://lccn.loc.gov/2022009729

All photographs taken by the author.
The following are illustrations by Alexander C. Williams:
Cover painting: "South Harbor, Essex, Connecticut"
Page 14: "Alex's vision of Mt. Eisenhower"
Page 32: "Motherhood in Nature"
Page 54: "The 'Spirit of St. Louis' over the Connecticut estuary, May 20, 1927"

Book design by Sarah Bauhan
Text set in Bembo Book Pro
Cover design by Henry James
Printed by Imprint Digital, Upton Pyne, Exeter, Devon

BAUHAN PUBLISHING LLC
PO BOX 117 PETERBOROUGH NEW HAMPSHIRE 03458
WWW.BAUHANPUBLISHING.COM   603-567-4430

Manufactured in the United Kingdom

In his 1905 book, *The Life of Reason*, the Harvard philosopher George Santayana (1863–1952) wrote: "The family is one of nature's masterpieces." Having grown up in a large family (eight siblings and twenty-five first cousins) and, with my wife Caroline, having created another (three children and ten grandchildren), I can attest to the validity of Professor Santayana's assertion.

Many of the essays in this collection incorporate family—a remembrance of a sister, hiking in the White Mountains, the passing of childhood, and memories of Christmases in years gone by. Families guide us in providing a moral compass. They inspire and comfort us. They share in our joy, and they provide love when life seems bleak. Life without family is unimaginable.

So, it is to all families, mine and yours, that this book is dedicated.

Sydney M. Williams III

August 2022

CONTENTS

Reflections

Literature

Acknowledgments

After assuming all responsibility for errors, whether of fact, grammar, or syntax, I want, first, to thank my grandson Alex Clay Williams. Despite carrying a full course load at Brandeis University and interning (virtually) with the Hayek Institute in Vienna, Alex, using his artistic talents, was able to find time to create the cover image and the drawings that accompany these essays.

This book would never have been possible without the expertise of Bauhan Publishing, specifically Sarah Bauhan, owner and publisher; Mary Ann Faughnan, editorial director, who corrected my many mistakes and suggested alterations that I should have considered; and Henry James, art director, who used his talents to create an attractive book. I respect and owe them more than they can possibly realize. Also, I want to thank Dick Shriver, publisher and editor of *Estuary* for allowing me to use the essay "The Connecticut—Meet the River," which was published in the Spring 2020 edition of that magazine.

While the writing of essays is personal, these pages would have been blank without the encouragement of family members and friends too numerous to mention. Deserving of special mention first is my wife Caroline who has been by my side for fifty-eight years. Next are my children: Sydney M. Williams IV, Caroline Featherston, and Edward Williams. While now in their fifties, they remain not just a joy, but they have become, along with their children (my grandchildren), inspirational. Their spouses—Beatriz Chantrill Williams, Bill Featherston, and Melissa Comer Williams—have provided advice when asked. I would also like to thank the hundreds of readers of my essays whose wisdom, reflections, and criticisms have improved my thinking and writing skills.

Introduction

My parents were artists, sculptors primarily, but painters as well. The art gene bypassed me; however, the writing of essays satisfies my creative impulses. E. B. White warned that in writing essays the author exposes himself, reminding me of the emperor's new clothes, but with a difference. While the Emperor paraded through town, naked as a jaybird, dressed in what he believed to be a suit of newly woven cloth visible only to the intelligent, the essayist, while keeping his privates private, exposes his soul.

I never wrote for a living but grew up in an age when people communicated through letters. I did take a course in journalism at the University of New Hampshire, and I had a job writing a sports column for *Foster's Daily Democrat*, a newspaper in Dover, New Hampshire. Twenty years ago, while working as a stockbroker in New York, I began writing a market note, as I could not understand prices then being paid for speculative, unseasoned technology companies. Those market notes morphed into essays on myriad subjects, from politics and family to nature and books.

This is my third collection, joining *One Man's Family* and *Notes from Old Lyme*, both published by Bauhan Publishing of Peterborough, New Hampshire, the town where I grew up. This book is special for me, as it includes a half dozen drawings by my talented grandson, Alex Williams, a senior at Brandeis University. The collection is divided into four sections: Nature and Family, Memories, Reflections, and Literature. They were written over the past dozen years. One of them, "The Connecticut—Meet the River," was previously published in *Estuary*, a quarterly magazine devoted to the Connecticut River and its watershed. It is reprinted with permission.

Ideas for essays appear often at night or when taking solitary walks, which requires keeping a pencil and paper handy. They are not sought. I never say to myself, Sydney, today you will write on the Monarch butterfly, tomorrow on a memory of working in Canada's Northwest

Territories, and the next day a piece on the joy of reading Wodehouse. All three are possible, but the process is serendipitous. Each essay is preceded by a rubric, which is supposed to capture the essence of what has been written. The essays range from 600 to over 3,000 words, with most being about 1,300 words—short enough to read in a few minutes and not so long as to bore . . . at least, that is my hope.

NATURE AND FAMILY

The fourteen essays in this section cover a geographic range from New Hampshire's White Mountains to an Essex, Connecticut, swamp. There is one on the death of my sister Charlotte, and another on the joys and wonders of motherhood, from the perspective of son, husband, father, and grandfather. The return of the Atlantic sturgeon to the Connecticut River prompted an essay. This section also includes the longest essay, "The Connecticut: Meet the River." Reading them, you will understand the importance to me of family, and that my love for the world around me exceeds my knowledge.

Alex's vision of Mount Eisenhower

New Hampshire's White Mountains
August 29, 2016

*Earth and sky, woods and fields, lakes and rivers, the mountains
and the sea are excellent school masters, and teach some of us
more than we can learn from books.*

Sir John Lubbock (1834–1913)
Naturalist, University of London

New Hampshire's mountains curl up in a coil.

Robert Frost (1874–1963)"New Hampshire," 1923

Straight ahead is Eisenhower. My eleven-year-old grandson George tells me the rounded, domed peak mimics the late president's bald head. I am impressed with his knowledge of past presidents. We are sitting on the veranda of the Mount Washington Hotel looking south and east toward the Presidential Range.

The hotel, now renovated and owned by the Omni Group, was the scene, in the summer of 1944, of the Bretton Woods Conference that set new rules for the postwar international monetary system, which created the International Monetary Fund (IMF) and assured stable currencies. The US dollar would remain exchangeable into gold at $35.00 per ounce. The system worked for twenty-seven years, until the Nixon Administration, coping with rising inflation and a run on the metal, ended gold convertibility in 1971.

In July of 1944 the Second World War had just over a year to run. By the time of the Conference the Allies had landed at Normandy. The Soviet Army was moving west toward the Elbe. American, British, and Canadian troops were pushing east toward the Rhine. Tens of thousands more would die, but ultimate victory seemed clear. Franklin Roosevelt and Winston Churchill, in the summer of 1944, were committed to avoiding what a lack of planning had unleashed on Europe in the years following the Armistice that ended the First World War twenty-six years earlier. Conference delegates were watched over by inspiring and magisterial peaks.

From our view on the veranda, we look out at a number of summits—

Pierce, Eisenhower, Franklin, Monroe, Washington, Reagan, Jefferson, Adams, and Madison. Franklin was named for Benjamin Franklin who, while never president, served a critical role in the founding of our government. There is a Mount Jackson, but that is named for Charles Thomas Jackson, a New Hampshire geologist, not Andrew Jackson. There is also a Mount Lincoln, but that is in Franconia Notch, not along the Presidential Range.

The White Mountain National Forest (WMNF) was established in 1918. While we typically associate Theodore Roosevelt with conservation efforts, it was President Benjamin Harrison who, in 1891, signed the bill creating the National Forest System. At 750,852 acres, the WMNF seems large, but relative to the 190 million acres of national forest owned by the federal government it is small. Geologists estimate that the White Mountains, which are part of the Appalachian Range, were formed about 100 million years ago. Even to a white-haired grandfather of ten that seems a long time ago. However, the Barberton Greenstone Belt in South Africa and the Hamersley Range in Australia date back three to five billion years.

The WMNF is a place to be enjoyed by all who venture north. A hundred miles of the Appalachian Trail, which extends from Springer Mountain in Georgia to Mount Katahdin in Maine, winds its way through and over peaks in New Hampshire's White Mountains. Eleven hundred miles of other trails make hiking in this preserve special. (My son, his wife, and their four children, who are staying with us, spent one day climbing the Ammonoosuc Ravine Trail, which begins near the base of the Cog Railway, to the top of Mount Washington.) One reason hikers return year after year is the possibility of membership in New Hampshire's restricted "4,000 Footers Club"—for those who have climbed New Hampshire's forty-eight peaks above 4,000 feet.

One of the more fascinating aspects of the White Mountains is the vegetation, and the changes one sees as one climbs through deciduous forests of maple and beech, to higher elevations, with birch, hemlock, red spruce, and balsam fir, into what is known as the Upper Boreal Zone (4,000 to 4,400 feet), and finally into the alpine region above tree line. (In the Upper Boreal Zone is an interesting plant, sphagnum moss. It is a green, bog moss with the feel of a damp sponge. During the First World War this moss was used as a field dressing for open wounds because it was sterile and capable of absorbing up to twenty times its volume in liquids.) Once above tree line, ground cover includes various sedges, grasses, and rushes, plants similar to those in the Arctic. Most peaks are windswept, thus devoid of any vegetation, apart from lichens that cling bravely to rocks and survive extreme cold and heavy snows. Clouds, which cover the Presidential Range 60 percent of the time, mean that moisture is greater the higher one climbs. Nevertheless, the soil is more acidic and contains fewer nutrients, as the mist washes restoratives down the mountain.

As a national forest, the White Mountains may be selectively logged, but its real purpose is as a place to be enjoyed by people for the beauty of its peaks, gorges, and vistas—to be at one with nature. Sitting on a ledge between Adams and Jefferson looking into the Great Gulf, or standing atop Madison looking south and west toward Washington one is reminded of man's relative insignificance. While there are wild animals like moose, black bears, white tail deer, and even the occasional bobcat, the risk to campers and hikers is the vastness of its space and, more especially, the weather. It is easy to get lost if one wanders off the trail, and the weather above tree line can change quickly. While mountains like Everest, Mount Blanc, or even Mounts Rainier and Hood in the United States are far higher and more difficult to climb, Mount Washington consistently ranks among the deadliest, because it gets more visitors and hikers are often surprised by high winds and low temperatures. Its modest height of 6,288 feet belies the ferociousness of its weather. Average wind speeds are in excess of forty miles per hour, with a record wind gust of 231 miles per hour recorded in April 1934. Temperatures in July and August average in the mid-forties, with frequent dips below freezing. More than 130 people have died on the mountain, generally because they were unprepared.

As we turn from the majestic view and return to the rest of our family, I realize George was right. Before being named Eisenhower in 1969, the peak was known as Dome Mountain, and before that Mount Pleasant—two words that, when used as adjectives, are appropriate to our thirty-fourth president. It makes me wonder: Where is a man like Ike today, and why, with mountains and ideals so high, have we descended so low?

Nature—Its Miracles and Mysteries
July 8, 2017

All the things of the universe are perfect miracles,
each as profound as any.

Walt Whitman (1819–1892)
"Proto-Leaf" (*Leaves of Grass*), 1860–1861

Being neither doctor nor scientist, I have the advantage of not dwelling on the mechanics of life; instead, I am awed by its mysteries and its miracles.

Among the most cherished miracles and mysteries of fatherhood is the introduction to one's newborn child—the marvel of its perfect toes with their beautifully formed nails, to the wisps of hair that sprout from its head. How did it come to be? How did it grow from an egg in the womb of my wife into this child I hold? How did it know when to leave the sanctity of that dark and comfortable place and enter the world, to be held at the breast of its mother? It is both a mystery and a miracle.

The Scottish philosopher and empiricist David Hume once defined a miracle as a "violation of the laws of nature." But 1,300 years earlier Saint Augustine wrote "miracles are not contrary to nature, but only contrary to what we know about nature." I think Saint Augustine got it right—experience and knowledge alone are not requirements for belief. I think of a miracle as an interpretation of an observation we do not understand—an explanation for something that cannot be explained—a mystery enshrouded in faith.

Walking the paths through the fields and woods that surround our home at Essex Meadows, I marvel at the interdependence of nature—of the fact that all forms of life—animals, birds, and fish—survive by consuming something that lives, or has lived and died. One ponders how life came to be. There is a chicken-and-egg aspect that is beyond my comprehension. Which came first? Scientists have theories, but I prefer the wonder of the unknown to the drudgery of the lab and the denseness of dusty texts. These are questions to put to philosophers, poets, and artists, as well as to doctors, scientists, and technicians. In breaking the analysis

Path through the woods at Essex meadows

down into rigid, mechanized component parts, do we not lose something of its mystery? Does science destroy imagination?

We look for perfection: "best-in-show" at the Westminster Kennel Club; a Triple Crown winner; the most perfect rooster, goat, sheep, cow, or the largest pumpkin and biggest tomato at a country fair. But perfection, like E. B. White's Stuart Little's search for Margalo, is a quest for castles in the air. All nature is a work in progress. It is a continuum. never finished. All life has evolved and will continue to do so.

Species adapt to changing environments, or they die. The evolutionary process for those whose lives are long, like man, is slow. A hundred years might produce three generations, hardly enough time to adapt if climate change comes quickly. On the other hand, the mayfly, which has a lifespan of twenty-four hours, would produce, in that same one hundred years, about 50,000 generations, allowing them to evolve as the environment changes.

Could we, I sometimes wonder as I meander under trees and across fields, with my field glasses and camera and in my shorts, sneakers, and baseball hat, survive in the wild? When we get hungry, we go to the supermarket. Fish, birds, and animals forage, or hunt and kill. When we are cold, we pull on a sweater. Birds that have stayed behind ruffle their feathers. Frogs bury themselves in the silt of streams and ponds beneath the ice. Many animals hibernate through cold winter nights. When we want to go somewhere, we get in our cars, trains, or buses. Our fellow creatures must fly, swim, walk, or slither. They, of necessity, are self-reliant. We change our clothes daily, something a cat—a stickler for cleanliness—must think frivolous. Most animals die wrapped in what they had been born in.

Nature is violent, but not in the way civilized man is. There are emotions we share: hunger, fear, surprise, and I suspect, loyalty and trust. Other emotions, such as lust, greed, hate, anger, and disgust—emotions responsible for senseless violence—are peculiar to man, not to the rabbits, turtles, and birds I see on my daily walks. I doubt there are any Hitlers or Stalins among the squirrels I watch leaping from branch to branch. Leopards and baboons are famous as mortal enemies, but I suspect it is not hatred that drives their need to battle, but fear and surprise. Neither employs experts, as we do, in places like the Pentagon or Znamenka 19 in Moscow, to map campaigns and plot the annihilation of enemies.

Most violence in nature is reserved for killing for food. Whether vegetarian or carnivorous, all creatures survive by eating something that is alive, or was. We may think it cruel on the unsuspecting frog to become breakfast for a black snake, but would we rather the snake starved? After all, the frog may have dined on a grasshopper the night before, the mother of whom was surely upset. And the snake, besides devouring moles we detest, provides fare for owls and hawks. This symbiosis in nature is one of its mysteries and its miracles. How did it come to be? Why does it work so well? Its complexity challenges today's most brilliant scientists. It is a system today's most sophisticated computer programmers could not reconstruct. This interdependency of species is one of life's miracles, its origin, a mystery.

Perhaps this is what is meant by taking time to "smell the roses," to appreciate nature around us. It's not necessary to understand every technical nuance, to provide the Latin name for every plant or animal, to deconstruct the scientific explanation as to why trees come alive in spring, or to question why beavers smack their tails when danger approaches. But it is important to be an observer, to appreciate nature in action—be it a honeybee gathering nectar, a chipmunk having lunch, a clutch of turtle eggs, or turkeys gathering their chicks as they scramble for cover. To see nature is to witness miracles. Best of all, it is a show without alpha or omega, and it is free. As Thomas Wolfe wrote, "Nature is the one place where miracles not only happen, but they happen all the time."

The Atlantic Sturgeon
May 18, 2017

Atlantic sturgeon didn't make it for 70 million years without being resilient.

Ted Williams
"Yale Environment 360"
Published by Yale School of Forestry and Environmental Studies
February 12, 2015

I attended a recent talk: "A Connecticut River Mystery Revealed," given by Kimberly Damon-Randall, a naturalist and administrator with NOAA (National Oceanic and Atmospheric Administration), at Essex Meadows. The subject: the Atlantic sturgeon, an ancient fish recently returned to the Connecticut River. The meeting was sponsored by the Roger Tory Peterson Estuary Center (RTPEC), on whose board I serve.

An old saying has it that they can kill you, but they can't eat you. Of course, a fish that is killed is usually eaten. The Atlantic sturgeon is desired especially for its eggs (caviar or "black gold" as they are known). The species is still with us, but man's rapacity over the past century severely limited its numbers. Fortunately, the fish was added to the Endangered Species Act in 2012 and is now making a comeback. However, as Mr. Williams (no relation) wrote in the article quoted above, the Atlantic sturgeon has been around for tens of millions of years, joining an exclusive club comprised of species like the horseshoe crab and the jellyfish, all of which learned to adapt. It survived the intense heat of the dinosaur age when temperatures averaged 20 percent higher than today. They made it through the ice age, which covered most of North America, Europe, and Asia with several hundred feet of ice. They survived the six-mile-wide Chicxulub asteroid, which hit the Yucatan Peninsula about sixty million years ago. Could man, with a brain that reasons and a mind that creates, have survived such devastation and extreme temperature changes? Given the dynamic earth on which we live, someday we will find out. Nevertheless, the Atlantic sturgeon adapted when most other animals with whom they lived during the Mesozoic Era did not.

The Atlantic sturgeon is primitive looking. Instead of having scales, it has five rows of bony plates, known as scutes. Its lifespan is about sixty years. At maturity, which is achieved between fifteen and twenty years, a female can weigh up to 800 pounds and be fifteen feet in length, an unusual sight in the estuary of the Connecticut River. The fish is anadromous, which means it migrates from salt water to spawn in fresh water, as do salmon, shad, and striped bass. It has an elongated snout, which differentiates it from its smaller, (and more common) cousin, the short-nose sturgeon. They are toothless, benthic omnivores. With a tube-like mouth located on the underside of the head, which extends several inches when feeding, they vacuum up insects, worms, clams, and mussels from sea- and riverbeds. Four barbels, which could be mistaken for fangs but are in fact taste buds, dangle from their upper lip. Like many of nature's creatures, they are camouflaged. Seen from above their brown coloring blends with the sea or river bottom, while their white belly, when viewed from below resembles the sky.

In early North America, Atlantic sturgeon were seen as a nuisance, as their rough skin would rip open fishing nets; but soon they became profitable—one of the first "cash crops" to be harvested in Jamestown, Virginia. Their exterior was used in clothing, bookbinding, and as isinglass. By the late nineteenth century, they were heavily fished for their eggs and flesh. Up to seven million pounds of sturgeon meat were exported annually in the last decade of the nineteenth century. But overfishing caused a sharp decline; exports declined to 22,000 pounds in 1920.

While its decline was precipitous; the Atlantic sturgeon's comeback has been gradual. According to the National Marine Fisheries Service (NMFS), in the late nineteenth century 180,000 "ripe" females entered the Delaware River annually (then known as the caviar capital of North America). Today, the agency estimates there are fewer than a hundred. Females reach sexual maturity about age sixteen and lay eggs every three to five years, so populations will rebound, albeit slowly.

Humans almost eradicated these fish a hundred years ago, and now humans are leading conservation efforts to restore them. It is their return to the Connecticut River that I find exciting. Three years ago, the remains of a seven-foot, one-hundred-pound immature female was found about five miles up the river, near the entrance to Hamburg Cove. In the same year (2014), a few pre-migratory juvenile specimens (estimated to have been hatched in 2013) were collected. DNA testing suggested that a small number of families—perhaps eleven—produced the offspring.

The fish found in 2014, according to the Connecticut Department of Energy and Environmental Protection (DEEP), were too small to have emigrated from other systems, so scientists felt certain they were hatched in the Connecticut River. It had been decades since such findings had been confirmed. Acoustic transmitters were implanted into a few larger fish, so that their movements can be tracked.

Spawning occurs in flowing waters, just beyond where the leading edge of seawater meets the fall line of freshwater—often near where dams have been built. A female can lay between 400,000 and eight million eggs, reaching maximum fertility at around thirty years of age. As a father of three children and grandfather of ten, that seems like a lot, but keep in mind, only a small percentage make it to adulthood. Eggs are easily destroyed, and the young serve as food for other species. As they get larger, and less appetizing to natural predators, survival probabilities increase. Besides man, not only as a fisherman but as a dredger and blaster of rock ledge, natural predators of mature Atlantic sturgeons include killer whales, sharks, and seals.

Generally, man operates in his own self-interest. In bygone times, and in primitive societies today, man did what he must to survive. Some of what he did was antithetical to modern concepts of conservation. However, we must keep in mind that conservation is a consequence of education and wealth. The first allows us to better know, understand, and appreciate our environment, while the second provides the funds necessary to preserve and conserve what we have inherited. We have come a long way in the past 150 years. Rivers are cleaner than they were, as is the air. About eighty-five million acres (3.5 percent of our land mass) is in national parks, with another fifteen million acres protected in land trusts. There remains work to be done, but we must balance the needs of all segments of society, so that the path we travel permits economic growth and conservation. Taken under our wings, to mix my metaphors, the Atlantic sturgeon should survive. I hope so, for it gives our children and grandchildren the opportunity to witness a species that lived during the time of the dinosaurs, a fascinating fact indicative of a remarkable resiliency. There is much we can learn from its adaptability to changing environmental conditions over many millennia.

The Joy of Grandchildren
January 14, 2018

*I love music of all kinds, but there is no greater music
than the sound of my grandchildren laughing.*

Sylvia Earle (1935–)
American marine biologist and author

On a recent visit to the home of my youngest granddaughter, a handwritten sign posted on the door leading from the mudroom to the kitchen read: "Manicure, one cent." Feeling the least a grandfather could do was encourage entrepreneurship, I consented to having my nails painted. Despite pleas that my nails not be varnished in some garish color, and the offer of a one-dollar bribe, I soon found myself with ten fingernails decorated as though they were Joseph's multicolored coat. A few hours later, and a penny and a dollar short, I walked into our home with my hands in my pockets, thinking of Ogden Nash: "When grandparents enter the door, discipline flies out the window."

Not everyone is fortunate to have grandchildren, so we count ourselves among God's chosen. We see in our grandchildren the promise and risks of the future—we dream of the places they will go, the people they will meet. We think of the loves and losses, joys and sadness, laughter and tears they will experience. We know they will learn from failure and that they will derive satisfaction from success. We know they will come to understand that work brings dignity and pride, and that they will have the chance to do those things we tried to do, and opportunities we missed.

While our lives lie in the past, theirs are the future. We have memories; they have the promise and mystery of the unknown. We look backward, sometimes cynically, through scrapbooks in the mind; they look forward, with hope and dreams. In their genes they carry our DNA, so we know a part of us will live forever.

Caroline and I have ten grandchildren. They are the issue of three sets of parents—all of whom were married within a twelve-month period—June 14, 1997, to June 20, 1998. Grandchildren (six girls and four boys) began arriving in 2000 and the wave did not stop until 2008. There was only one year—2007—when the stork didn't deliver a new package.

Today, two of them are high school juniors and three high school sopho-mores. The rest scale down to the fourth grade.

Time goes by faster as we age, so the speed with which they left be-hind cribs, diapers, and Santa Claus has been startling. One moment they looked up to me as the fount of all wisdom. Now, they look down at me and kindly ask if they might help me with my iPhone. It seems only yesterday I was pushing them in a stroller. Now, I hurry to keep up. Was it only a decade ago, I was reading bedtime stories? Now, they want to discuss quantitative physics, the New York Giants offensive line, and the situation in Ukraine.

Like all grandchildren, mine like to hear stories—what it was like in the "olden" days. Former poet laureate (and New Hampshire resident) Donald Hall wrote about haying with his grandfather in the 1930s: "Even more I loved the slower plod back to the barn. My grandfather told story after story with affection and humor." Mine like to hear what it was like to grow up in the 1940s and 1950s—music we listened to, books we read, games we played, clothes we wore, food we ate, schools we attended. They want to understand what it was like to live without computers, fast-food restaurants, iPhones, or Amazon. They ask questions, as I did of my grandparents, trying to understand what it was like to live in a differ-ent time. While attention spans are short, they hear me, just as I heard my grandparents seventy years ago. What is difficult to comprehend is try-ing to foresee the stories they will tell their grandchildren, seventy years hence. Will their childhoods seem as primitive to their grandchildren as mine is to them, and my grandparents' childhoods were to me?

Their activities reflect the eternality of sports, the enduring appeal of extracurricular programs, and the timelessness of youth: playing on the beach, swing sets, and Little League. And now a multiplicity of sports and activities: squash, tennis, lacrosse, horseback riding, soccer, cross-coun-try, track, skiing, and swimming. One grandson tutors students whose first language is not English. One granddaughter is an Irish dancer, and another is captain of her school's squash team. Another grandson plays the cello and a granddaughter the violin. Two grandchildren are in school choirs. Two are accomplished artists, and one has written a yet-unpub-lished novel. A granddaughter volunteers at a riding academy for children with physical disabilities, and a grandson in Amnesty International. Two have had summer jobs as camp counselors. We have watched our oldest

A Covid Christmas in a Darien garage, 2021

granddaughter play in a New England squash tournament in Deerfield, Massachusetts, and her cousin play lacrosse for Darien, Connecticut's high school. Two granddaughters take riding lessons, and I have witnessed their improving horsemanship. We have watched two grandsons wallop tennis balls, and others swim, play soccer, lacrosse, squash, and run cross-country. They enjoy being young and are beginning to experience the emotional traumas of the teen years. All ten are fortunate to have loving parents in stable families. All ten live relatively close to their needy grandparents.

I live vicariously through them, feeling the ball hit my racquet, the muscles of the horse beneath the saddle, the splash of water in my face, and the sliding of my skis across the snow. I think, this is why we are here.

Having grandchildren recalls time I spent with my grandparents. Mine were born between 1873 and 1888. They grew up before cars or telephones—something improbable to my grandchildren who will ride around in driverless cars and speak into wristwatch phones. I remember thinking my grandparents were from another age—gas street lamps, electricity-free homes, horse-drawn street cars—real-life figures that leapt from dusty text books. I knew I would learn from them, and I instinctively knew I was special to them. I loved to hear stories of cows driven down Boston's Beacon Street, carriages on Hillhouse Avenue in New Haven, and life on a tobacco farm in Tennessee. Grandparents are to be treasured.

My youngest grandson made a disparaging comment about Communism. He was asked by his well-read older brother: "Do you even know what Communism is?" "Yes, I do. It's when two people work, one for two hours and the other for ten hours, and they both get paid the same." There was enough truth in his answer that I don't worry about their generation. They know how the world works. As I think about my grandchildren, the lyrics of Bob Dylan's song come to mind:

> *May your heart always be joyful;*
> *May your song always be sung;*
> *And, may you stay forever young.*

My message to my grandchildren: You will encounter storms; you will be becalmed; you will face anger and jealousy but also love and forgiveness. With eyes on the horizon, you will reach shore. And take comfort in the fact that your grandparents—your perfectly correct grandmother and your politically incorrect grandfather—love you unconditionally.

Autumn Evenings
October 1, 2002

Youth is like spring, an over praised season,
more remarkable for biting winds than genial breezes.

Autumn is the mellowed season,
and what we lose in flowers we more than gain in fruits.

The Way of all Flesh
Samuel Butler (1835–1902)
Published posthumously, 1903

The bright evening sun casts long shadows across the lawn, pasture, and marsh on the first autumn weekend of the year. Fall began this year with the autumnal equinox on September 20 and will end three months later with the winter solstice, when the sun arcs through the southernmost part of the sky. Here, at the mouth of the Connecticut River, nighttime on that day will exceed daylight by five hours. On another evening, light and dark clouds compete for dominance in the fading twilight. The river, reflecting the last of the sun's rays, turns white from the blue of the sky it had reflected only a few minutes earlier.

Fall is my favorite season. Days are warm, and nights are cool. It is the one time of the year when the thermostat can be set to the "off" position. The season begins with trees clad in their dress of green. It ends with limbs barren, but not lifeless. Leaves, through which deciduous trees receive and store energy, lose their purpose and so turn color as they die and fall in glorious piles that are only a nuisance in afterthought. When I was young my father would gather leaves and press them against the foundation of the house. In death they had value as insulation. Today, unable to burn what is already dead, we send them to landfills. In the meantime, the trees hibernate, conserving strength for spring's resurrection.

The red maples and the dogwoods are the first to turn color, beginning in the waning days of September. Even the leaves of our lonely but stately American elm, our sole survivor of what was once a proud Connecticut species, begin to turn color early in October. The tall, superior-looking sugar maples hold off for another few weeks. Of course, the holly and coniferous trees stay green all winter, providing color against the bleakness of the season. Flowerbeds persist into October, refusing to say "uncle," while the rugosa roses bloom into early November, when they are cut down to get them through winter's snow and cold. They will grow even more abundant next year.

Marsh grasses fold over and turn brown, dulling the landscape, and the river takes on a grey and steely look. Nevertheless, the warmth of long summer days has kept the water temperature warmer than the air, the opposite of what happens in the spring. It is a great time to kayak, with falling leaves leaving more of the riverbank exposed.

For farmers, autumn is the time to harvest what was sown half a year earlier. For many of the birds that summer on these shores, it is the time to head south, to the warmth of southern nests, leaving behind downy woodpeckers and black-capped chickadees that stay through the winter. For squirrels, it is a time for gathering foods that will see them through months of hibernation. The deer, of necessity, become bolder, showing up on the lawn where grass and bushes provide sustenance. Since the first Thanksgiving, fall is the time when Americans give thanks for the boun- ty that land and nature provide, which they pray will see them through to spring's renewal.

In a lyrical but poignant first novel, *In the Shadow of the Banyan*, Vaddey Ratner captures the spirit of rebirth. She writes of her own experiences surviving Cambodia's killing fields during the Khmer Rouge nightmare years of 1975 to 1979: "And since then, I'd learned to see things not as they were, but for what they meant—that even when it rained, the sun could still shine, and the sky might offer something infinitely more beautiful than white clouds and blue expanse, that colors could burst forth in the most unexpected moment." The gathering of crops and falling leaves; the birds flying south, and animals going into hibernation are all characteri- zations of autumn, yet they hold the promise of spring.

Many equate the seasons with life's progress, suggesting that people my age are in their autumnal years. But I prefer to look past the seasons, knowing that much of what dies today will regenerate in a few months. It is what gives life a sense of the eternal. In my case, I look at my grand- children and see my future. It is the promise of rebirth that makes autumn so beautiful.

Autumn evening in the Connecticut River's estuary

Motherhood in nature

Motherhood
August 9, 2017

Sometimes the strength of motherhood is greater than natural laws.

Barbara Kingsolver (1955–)
American novelist, essayist, and poet

*Each child is biologically required to have a mother. Fatherhood is
a well-regarded theory, but motherhood is a fact.*

P. J. O'Rourke (1947–2022)
Political satirist and journalist

A late spring day a few years ago: The car in front of me has stopped. I am on Neck Road, a hundred yards north of Smith Neck Road in Old Lyme. The woman who had been driving is standing outside her car. On the side of the road, a fawn stands on three legs—the fourth dangling uselessly . . . and painfully. It is the mother deer, the doe, that grips my attention. She stands helplessly, a few yards away, unable to do anything. Instinct (and devotion?) would not let her seek safety. Mothers are mothers, no matter the species.

Obviously, I have no firsthand experience of motherhood, but I have a lot of secondhand knowledge. I am the grandson of two mothers, the son of a mother, husband to a mother, brother to four sisters who are mothers, father to a daughter who is a mother, and father-in-law to two daughters-in-law who are mothers. I have six granddaughters who I pray will someday be mothers. As a child growing up with horses, goats, chickens, dogs, and cats, I have witnessed innumerable births. Caroline and I had a goat that gave birth to two kids, and we had cats that had kittens. I have witnessed mothers in the wild.

"But first and foremost, I remember Mama." That is the opening sentence of Katrin Hanson's story, *Mama and the Hospital*, and the closing line of the movie, *I Remember Mama*. For those of us of a certain age, Irene Dunne, as Marta Hanson, epitomized motherhood. She played Mama, the mother of a poor Norwegian immigrant family in 1910 San Francisco. She was the glue that held them together. We identify with this hard-working, devoted woman who so adored her children that she once took a job mopping floors in a hospital so that she could visit her patient-child.

Mothers abound in literature; not all are good ones. Remember Medea who skewers her child because her husband Jason wants to take a new wife, or Prince Hamlet's mother Gertrude who marries her husband's killer, Claudius? Or what about Joan Crawford, as depicted by her adopted daughter Christine, in *Mommie Dearest*? On the other hand, many mothers in literature are good. Recall the Biblical story of the two harlots, and how Solomon discerned the right mother? Then there is Mary, mother of Jesus, and Hester Prynne, heroine of Nathaniel Hawthorne's *The Scarlet Letter*. We read of the socially clumsy Mrs. Bennet in Jane Austen's *Pride and Prejudice*, and Scarlett O'Hara who was torn between her real mother and her Mammy in *Gone with the Wind*, a subject Kathryn Stockett wrote of decades later in *The Help*. The most tortured mother in literature, in my reading, was Sophie Zawistowski, the eponymous heroine of William Styron's novel *Sophie's Choice*. Sophie, with her two young children, as we learn toward the end of the novel, was taken to Auschwitz, where she was confronted by an SS officer: "You may keep one of your children. The other one will have to go. Which one will you keep?"

It is often said that men marry women like their mother. People who knew my mother and know my wife would be unable to see the similarities, except in one important way—both raised happy and successful children. In my unbiased opinion, our children were fortunate in their mother.

A mother has instinctual love for the child she has borne, a sense foreign to fathers. As Karen Rinaldi recently wrote in an op-ed in *The New York Times*, fathers sometimes complain about having to "babysit" their children. However, she notes: "Has a woman ever 'babysat' her own children?" It is not that as fathers we do not love our children. We do. But we do not have the same intuitive love as does a mother when she first clutches to her breast a living, breathing being that moments before had been in her womb. We see that in the bitch as she licks clean her newborn pups, and in the mare as she gently helps her newborn foal to her feet. It is not cruelty when a mother bird nudges her young out of the nest to test her or his wings. Even instincts that we might see as barbarous are usually acts of survival—chickens will sometimes eat eggs whose shells are deficient in calcium, and polar bears will sometimes kill and devour the smallest of their young. A friend who has a farm in Provence recently told me that his goose, who hatched two goslings (when one is typical), was not overwrought when a hawk took away the smallest.

Love for a newborn is eternal. In *Bleak House*, Charles Dickens wrote of Lady Dedlock when she first realized that the little girl who she thought had died in her first moments was alive: "O my child, my child! Not dead in the first hours of her life, as my cruel sister told me; but sternly nurtured by her, after she had renounced me and my name! O my child, my child!"

Being mothers has not impeded women from careers. History is replete with those who have done both: Abigail Adams, Sojourner Truth, Julia Ward Howe, Marie Curie, Elizabeth Cady Stanton, and Indira Gandhi. Far more have careers today: Hillary Clinton, Nikki Haley, J. K. Rowling, Sheryl Sandberg, and my daughter-in-law, the author Beatriz Williams. In fact, today's labor participation rate is higher for mothers (70.5 percent) than for the workforce as a whole (62.8 percent). Nevertheless, motherhood takes effort and time. It takes an understanding of newborns. As they grow, mothers teach them to fledge, swim on their own, feed, and fear predators. In humans, mothers are first responders in loving and nurturing their children to become productive, responsible citizens who will, in time, love and nurture their own children.

In some quarters, the concept of motherhood is under attack, or, at least, not being accorded the respect it deserves. Over the past several decades, young people in Western societies have delayed marriage and children. Getting a good education, starting a career, building financial independence, and the desire to prove one's independence—all valid explanations—are cited as reasons women choose to delay childbirth. The consequences in developed nations have been birth rates below what is necessary to sustain population without immigration.

Since Thomas Malthus, in the late eighteenth century, warned that population growth was exceeding agriculture's ability to sustain it, Cassandras have repeatedly warned that the planet is overcrowded. For over two hundred years, doomsayers have been proved wrong. Will they be right at some point? Perhaps. But what economists and prophets ignore is the creativity and industriousness of men and women—how productive they have made the land and how their innovation has made lives more comfortable. We should not disregard the limits of nature's resources, but we should respect our abilities to conceive, create, and adapt. Conception, keep in mind, is the ultimate expression of optimism.

In the *Times* article quoted above, Karen Rinaldi, an author and founder of the Harper Wave imprint of Harper Collins, wrote, "Motherhood is not a sacrifice, but a privilege." I agree, but it is more. In passing one's genes to the next generation, motherhood may be selfish, as Ms. Rinaldi asserted, but that is not the thought I would have had, and "privilege" is not the only word I would have used to describe motherhood. In my opinion, birth is a blessing of divine proportions. When we consider the odds against being born—the right sperm and the right egg at the right time—it is as much a miracle as a physical happening. Science has made giving birth safer and easier, but it has neither altered the process nor changed the consequence. Motherhood is also a duty. Without it, we would become extinct.

Motherhood, as my wife reminds me, is above all an emotional challenge. Good mothers understand the awesome responsibility that is theirs—that, in bringing into the world a new life, they must ensure that the baby they bore, the child they reared, the teenager they argued with and advised, becomes a self-sufficient, caring, respectful, responsible, and productive adult. Motherhood is unlike any other experience. There is nothing that equals it in importance. Jeff Bezos may have more money than anyone else. Wernher von Braun may have developed the mathematical models that put man on the moon. Elon Musk may have conceived a Hyperloop allowing one to travel between New York and Washington in twenty-nine minutes. But none could bear a baby. None can create the future. None can claim motherhood—a miraculous privilege, duty, and responsibility, critical to all species.

Murmuration of Swallows
October 17, 2017

True hope is swift, and flies with swallow's wings.

William Shakespeare (1564–1616)
Richard III, Act 5, Scene 2, 1592

They began to arrive a few minutes before dusk—a few singly, many in small groups, then larger, as the sun sank toward the horizon. Soon the darkening sky was laden with tens of thousands of tree swallows. They swept and dove in unison, first in one direction, then in another—sonar infallible, as they flew inches apart at speeds of up to forty miles per hour. They circled, then twirled earthward at ever increasing speeds, in tornado-like formation, to the grasses on Goose Island, just off Old Lyme, in the Connecticut River.

What we witnessed was one of nature's magical moments. Ornithologists know why swallows stop to feed—to bulk up for the long migration south. They understand why they congregate in "flights." There is safety in numbers, against peregrine falcons, red-tailed hawks, and other predators. Naturalists know that the dense stands of phragmites on Goose Island provide protection against predators. They also realize that the Connecticut River's estuary offers a high-density population of crepuscular insects for feeding. But scientists don't know how the birds' sonar works—what allows them to fly in close formation, while changing direction, without colliding.

Around the world there are more than eighty types of swallows, with Africa carrying the largest numbers. They are found throughout North America, with tree, barn, cave, cliff, and bank swallows among the most common. They, along with martins, belong to the family of passerine birds, known for aerial feeding.

Murmuration describes the phenomenon of birds flying in formation, swooping first one way and then another, in perfect harmony. The word derives from Middle English, the act of murmuring—the utterance of low, continuous sounds, or complaining noises. Listening carefully, as we watched them gather and circle before their descent, the noise was detectable. Swallows are not alone in their ability to fly in synchronized fashion.

Starlings, often seen as one of nature's least-loved birds, are known for their aerial acrobatics—again, mostly to avoid predators, like falcons or hawks. It is difficult for a bird of prey to single out an individual starling or swallow when the group is moving in unison, inches apart. Keep in mind, as well, flocking birds are not idle. They eat on the fly. They roost to rest. Scientists have determined that individual starlings are able to consistently coordinate with their seven nearest neighbors, yet how hundreds collectively correlate such movements, while flying wingtip-to-wingtip, remains a mystery.

The Connecticut River estuary is not the only place where swallows perform these ballets. They can be seen in the fall in England, before flying 3,500 miles to South Africa. Floridians see them in the spring, before they make their way north. Like most living things, swallows are creatures of habit. For many years, cliff swallows summered at the Mission in San Juan Capistrano, California, building nests in the old stone church. For eighty years, their return was celebrated on March 19. Then, in the 1990s, when workers removed their nests during restoration of the Mission, the swallows were forced to find alternative accommodations, including a near-by housing project. Now they are being wooed back with fake nests and the playing of recorded vocalizations. This past spring a few mud nests began to appear. The celebrations will continue.

The Old Lyme gathering—ours that is, not the swallows—was at a beautiful home, overlooking Goose Island, a few hundred yards offshore—all in the estuary of the Connecticut River—and no more than a couple of miles from where Roger Tory Peterson lived for over forty years. Kayakers and other boaters could be seen positioning themselves, as they do each night for about a week when swallows descend to this small island—stuffing their bodies and conserving their strength—before continuing the long flight south. A high school string quartet played softly in the back ground, the music drifted through the evening air, as friends chatted, sipped wine, and munched on passed hors d'oeuvres. All of us marveled at what we had witnessed. How lucky we are to live in this place.

It is the job of scientists to seek answers. There is still much for them to study; for example, the nerve systems that allow birds their remarkable sonar. But for the rest of us, the beauty is in the mystery—the fascination of watching, without comprehending, the murmuration of swallows.

Nature is humbling. How does something we cannot explain—cannot even fathom—function? In this natural world with its beauty and complexities, there is room for both the artist and the scientist, each of whom, in their own way, seeks understanding.

Pigs in Transit
June 1, 2016

Trust me Wilbur, people are very gullible. They'll believe anything they see in print.

E. B. White (1899–1985)
Charlotte's Web, 1952

During the late 1990s and early 2000s, when Caroline and I lived in bucolic splendor on Smith's Neck in Old Lyme, Connecticut, we kept two pigs. They were seasonal—they arrived in the spring as piglets and departed in the fall as full-grown hogs. It was a symbiotic relationship. We fed them for six months; they fed us for six months—nature at work. Caroline and I, of course, got the better of the bargain.

We were fortune that a good friend lived on our property who acted as "pigman." It is an honorable profession, made famous by P. G. Wodehouse in his Blandings stories. Like his fictional predecessors, George Cyril Wellbeloved, James Pirbright, and Monica Simmons, Lenny lovingly cared for the pigs. He delivered them as little squealers, ensured they were well-fed and watered, and then, at the end of six months, carted them—reluctantly—to their final point of departure in Salem, Connecticut. Capital and labor split the spoils evenly. Like Wodehouse's "Empress of Blandings," our pigs lived well, though ours remained nameless. We could not call a pig "Wilbur" in May and have him (or her) for breakfast in December. Their pen, which was about five hundred yards from the house, had a beautiful view of the Connecticut River and Long Island Sound. It was one of my favorite destinations on weekends. Unlike Lord Emsworth who was tall and droopy, I could not drape my shorter, stouter frame across the fence that enclosed our pig emporium . . . but I tried.

"Dakota," our black lab/golden retriever combination, was fascinated with the pigs. She would spend hours circling and sniffing their home. The fence around the sty was solid and too tall for her to see over. However, early on she discovered a knot hole at eye level. She would spend hours watching them with her one good eye. If I went to the other side of the pen, I could see that inquiring eye tracking their movements. She saw them grow from smaller than herself to considerably larger.

Pigs are intelligent animals, as George Orwell described in *Animal*

Farm—ranging just behind great apes, dolphins, and elephants in brain power. For example, I was amazed at how quickly they learned to get water flowing by pressing their snouts against a water pipe. Pigs are used for medical research, as they share common characteristics with us—similar chest and abdominal muscles, along with thoracic and abdominal organs. Embryonic pigs were used for dissection purposes when I was in high school biology class. With an estimated two billion pigs in the world (and seventy-three different breeds) there is little danger of them becoming endangered, even with 115,000,000 being slaughtered every year. Not to worry—the average sow gives birth to just under twenty piglets a year, a replacement rate not seen in most large mammals. Pigs are a big business. Circle Four Farms in Milford, Utah, for example, raises and markets 1.2 million pigs a year. Its parent company Smithfield Foods produces six billion pounds of pork a year. Ours was a boutique operation.

Pigs live in a variety of environments, from tropical rainforest in Southeast Asia to the icy cold of Siberia. Pot-bellied Vietnamese pigs are kept as pets. Domesticated pigs in Europe known as truffle hogs are used to ferret out that delicacy. Despite a reputation as being dirty—pigs love to wallow in mud to keep cool—they are remarkably clean animals. They have the misfortune, though, to incorporate within their rounded bodies delicacies we love, and they inhabit a world where most men can still outwit a pig.

History tells us that China was home to the first domesticated pigs six thousand years ago. And the pig remains one of the twelve animals in the Chinese Zodiac. They represent fortune, honesty, happiness, and fertility. Hernando DeSoto is credited with bringing the first swine to the new world in 1539. They have stocky bodies, small eyes, large ears, and short, curly tails. Winston Churchill liked pigs. He once said: "Dogs look up to man. Cats look down on man. Pigs look us straight in the eye and see an equal." But it was hard for me to look our pigs in the eye, as I knew their fate.

Our pigs arrived weighing twenty to thirty pounds. Some might call them cute, but they were obviously pigs. Ours were American Yorkshires. Over the course of the summer and early fall they would add a hundred and fifty pounds. Good food, a relaxed atmosphere, and little strenuous exercise made for contented pigs—at least during their short lives. As summer turned to fall and the leaves changed color and the first frost was felt, I knew their days were numbered. I would walk down to the sty, lean on the fence, toughen my mind, straighten my spine, and ponder on the fact that what I was seeing would soon become a freezer filled with rashers, sausages, chops, and roasts. Such thoughts made easier any feelings of guilt I had. Before freezing nights would cause water in the pipes to burst, Lenny would back his truck up to the pen. A ramp, sprinkled with corn, would be lowered that led from the pen to the bay of the truck. The unsuspecting pigs simply followed their snouts. By the time they realized where they were, it was too late. Lenny was already driving them north.

Only once was I able to watch this final act. Even though nameless, they were not anonymous. I had spent too many hours observing them, witnessing their camaraderie, watching them dig into the cool, damp soil on hot, muggy days, sleeping away others. It was sad to see them go, but I knew that what would return would be neatly packaged and taste delicious.

All living things must die. In *Charlotte's Web*, E. B. White has Charlotte say to Wilbur, as she is dying: "After all, what's a life anyway? We are born, we live a little while, we die." Well, life is more than that. It is true that we, like our pigs, live our lives in transit. But, if we leave the world better than we found it, if we provide something for others after we are gone, we have done some good. Wilbur felt that way about Charlotte. Our pigs set a similar example. Their lives had meaning, as our filled freezer would attest. And our lives were enhanced by their presence.

Mud River Swamp
May 24, 2017

Hope and the future for me are not in lawns and cultivated fields, not in towns and cities, but in the impervious and quaking swamps.

Henry David Thoreau (1817–1862)
"Walking," a lecture, 1851

In the musical *The Sound of Music*, Julie Andrews' character sings: "The hills are alive with the sound of music." Just as truthfully, but less poetically, one could say that from Mud River Swamp comes the cacophony of an untutored symphony. "In all swamps, the hum of mosquitoes drowns this modern hum of society," wrote Henry David Thoreau in his journal. The Mud River Swamp abounds with nature in its roughly twenty acres. The evensong of peepers is a harbinger of spring. Every so often, during late winter nights, comes the howl of coyotes and the hoots of the eastern screech-owl. On spring mornings, we wake to the song of the catbird. But it is during spring, summer, and early fall days that the swamp is audibly alive. At night beavers build, skunks hunt, and predators prey. With daylight come the sounds of birds, insects, and frogs, comprising an undisciplined but intoxicating orchestra. Flutes and clarinets compete with violins and cellos, only to be interrupted by French horns and the clash of cymbals. Combined, they produce a noise that would make Beethoven wince, but there is magic in its variety.

The word "swamp" is often spoken with a sneer. We think of the one in Washington that needs draining, or the demeaning term "swamp Yankees," which refers to tight-fisted New Englanders. For others, the word conjures thoughts of slime, unpleasant smells, places difficult to penetrate and land that has no commercial value. But it was from swamps that life sprang. Water is life's genesis. From the Old Testament, we learn of the importance of the Tigris–Euphrates wetlands, and of the Fertile Crescent, through which the two rivers flow south and east, from the Zagros Mountains on the Turkey–Iraq border, through Syria and Iraq, to the Persian Gulf. It was from this part of the world that human history was first recorded.

Thoreau, an admirer of swamps, wrote: "I derive more of my subsistence from the swamps which surround my native town than from the cultivated gardens in the village." He added, ". . . hope and the future for me are not in lawns and cultivated fields, not in towns and cities, but in the impervious and quaking swamps." In his most famous work, *Walden*, he acknowledges swamps' critical role in nature and of mankind's dependence on them: "Without the wetland, the world would fall apart. The wetland feeds and holds together the skeleton of the body of nature."

"A swamp," noted David Carroll in his 1999 book, *Swampwalker's Journal*, "is a wetland forest of tall trees, living or dead, standing in still-water pools or in drifting floods of water, or rising from seasonally saturated earth." All swamps, whether coastal or inland, have in common sufficient water and poor drainage. Dead trees, common enough in swamps, are a boon for woodpeckers whose homes bedeck their trunks. Insects, like ants, feed on the tissues that connect roots to the crown. It is the oxygen-depleted water of swamps that causes the roots of most trees to die. An exception is the alder. In his book, *The Hidden Life of Trees*, Peter Wohlleben noted this phenomenon: "Their secret [alders] is a system of air ducts inside their roots. These [ducts] transport oxygen to the tiniest tips, a bit like divers who are connected to the surface via a breathing

Mud River, Essex, Connecticut

tube." Swamps are transition areas that provide natural and valuable eco-logical services, like flood control, water purification and carbon storage; they serve as wildlife habitats. Coastal swamps are spawning areas for fish. The largest swamp in the world is the Pantanal floodplain of the Amazon River, which lies mostly in Brazil, but also reaches into Bolivia and Paraguay. It encompasses seventy thousand square miles, roughly the size of North Dakota. In the United States, the Atchafalaya Swamp, at the lower end of the Mississippi, is the United States' largest swamp. Most fa-mous of our swamps is the Everglades, a six-thousand square mile system that comprises the "River of Grass," which has its origin in the Kissim-mee River near Orlando and empties into the Straits of Florida.

My swamp (to inaccurately use the possessive) is the Mud River Swamp. (The swamp has no name. I felt that an oversight on the part of the cartographers, so I named it after the brook that runs through it.) It consists of about twenty acres, located within Essex Meadows' one hun-dred acres. The Mud River is no more than a trickle when it descends from The Preserve, a thousand-acre property of protected forest that abuts Essex Meadows. The ten-foot drop over a hundred-feet is grandilo-quently called a cascade. The stream then relaxes, as it gently meanders and widens out, among willows, alders, skunk cabbage, and mosses that make their homes here.

The Mud River heads east and then north where it intersects with the Fall River, about two miles away. The Fall River wends east another mile or so, until it enters the Connecticut at North Cove in Essex. At its head-waters, I watch the brook slip over the rocks in the cascade, knowing that its waters will mix with those of the Connecticut, a river that runs four hundred miles from the Canadian border to Long Island Sound. I think of the beavers that build dams, to give themselves a home, and I wonder about the fish that swim in it. I rejoice in the birds whose songs mingle with the sound of trickling waters and the deer that drink from it, and I am thankful for the otters and muskrats that play along its banks.

Water is where life began. Bill Nye, the science guy, says that in our search for alien life, "the presence of water is key." In his *Swampwalker's Journal*, David Carroll wrote: "Although I know of the oceanic origins of life on earth, it is in swamps and marshes that I feel my keenest sense of life's past, my sharpest intimations of life's journey in time, and my own moment within the ongoing." Swamps are ancient, something

P. G. Wodehouse knew. He had Bertie Wooster muse in *The Inimitable Jeeves*, ". . . on the occasions when Aunt is calling to Aunt, like mastodons bellowing across primeval swamps. . . ."

There is death in swamps. Many creatures live off the flesh of another that has died, while others dine on greens like grasses, plants, and berries. The coyote, the largest predator known to feed in our swamp, eats muskrats, otters, ducks, snakes, frogs, turtles, and even a beaver. His victims, in turn, eat smaller creatures, like minnows, worms, and insects. Nature is symbiotic. Even the smallest creature deserves our attention and concern, as Shakespeare reminded us in *Measure for Measure*:

> *The poor beetle, which we tread upon,*
> *In corporal sufferance finds a pang as great,*
> *As when a giant dies.*

My swamp is a way-place for migrating birds, as well as home for dozens of avian species who build nests within its trees and bulrushes. On a recent bird walk, on a chilly day in May, we identified thirty species, either by sight or sound. And that did not include a mallard drake that I often watch protecting his nesting hen. We did not see the red-tailed hawk I often see searching for mice or chipmunks, nor did we sight the owl we sometimes hear at night. We did, though, see or hear red-winged blackbirds, yellow warblers, downy woodpeckers, and cedar waxwings, among others.

Swamps are like our cities. Thousands of species and millions of individuals live within their borders. Most of the sounds we hear are either mating calls or warnings to intruders. Violence and murder are common in swamps, perhaps more so than in our cities. But greed, hatred, jealousy, or revenge are never the motives. The death of one means life to another. Thoreau saw that, and he inverted Christian orthodoxy, claiming that in the midst of death we are in life.

We are fortunate to live on the edge of this swamp. Man has used nature for his own purposes. We have fished its waters, cultivated its fields, mined its minerals, chopped down its trees, diverted its wetlands, built dams along rivers to generate power, harnessed its tides and winds, and captured its sunlight. In doing so, we have become wealthy; and that wealth allows us to give back. We need to be conscious that, while most resources are renewable, there is a limit to what we can do, and that "renewable" can mean millions of years. The world is in constant motion.

We cannot ask it to stand still, but we can conserve what we have—let nature takes its course, with us leaving minimal footprints. We must be mindful that it is the ability to adapt to changing environmental conditions, regardless of their cause, that allows species to evolve. In a quote that is applicable to extremists on both ends of the environmental spectrum, E. B. White once wrote: "I would feel more optimistic about a bright future for man if he spent less time proving he can outwit Nature and more time tasting her sweetness and respecting her seniority."

I am neither a scientist nor a naturalist, but I love the world we live in. I walk around the Mud River swamp, ignorant of the names of most of the creatures and trees that I see, but that neither reduces my appreciation, nor diminishes my respect. We don't have to travel far to see marvels of nature. With eyes and ears open, there are millions of stories for us to witness. You have your swamp, and I have mine, in the Mud River.

The Connecticut—Meet the River
June 15, 2019

'This river, what is it called?' Balty asked the ferryman.
'We calls it the Great River. Which it be.'

Christopher Buckley (1952–)
The Judge Hunter, 2018
(story takes place in 1664)

The word "Connecticut" stems from a French corruption of the Mohegan word "Quinetucket," which means "beside the long tidal river." Adriaen Block, the Dutch explorer and first European to chart the river in 1614, called it the Fresh River. The English first settled the area in the 1630s and referred to it as the Great River. During the next couple of decades, the English moved west from the Massachusetts Bay Colony and north up the river, forcing the Dutch to retreat westward to New Haven, which was settled in the 1640s. By 1654, the English–Dutch boundary was established near what is now Greenwich, separating the Connecticut Colony from the New Netherland Colony (New York). During those years, the Great River began to be called the Connecticut, as was the colony established along its banks.

The Connecticut River begins its 406-mile trip to the sea in Pittsburg, New Hampshire. The iconic town was described by David Duncan in a 1985 piece for *The New York Times*: "Pittsburg (population 832) is a lazy village that in 1832 was the capital of a short-lived nation, the Indian Stream Republic, which drew up its own constitution and elected a president during border disputes between Canada and New Hampshire." The river has its origin in the Fourth Connecticut Lake, just above Moose Head Dam and three hundred yards from the Canada–United States border, a boundary fixed by the 1783 Treaty of Paris that ended the Revolutionary War. Over its long run to the sea, the river descends 2,670 feet, with a watershed that spans five of the New England states (including Maine, briefly) and the Canadian province of Quebec. The watershed encompasses 7.2 million acres (twice the size of the state of Connecticut) and includes one hundred and forty-eight tributaries, on which once sat three thousand dams and over which there are forty-four thousand crossings.

Ninety percent of its watershed is undeveloped, with only 200,000 acres (3 percent) in conservation. Over two million people live in the three hundred and fifty communities along its banks. The Connecticut begins its journey in a southwesterly direction before hitting the New Hampshire–Vermont border, then heads pretty much due south, until the "big bend" just south of Middletown, Connecticut, where it flows southeasterly until it reaches Long Island Sound between Old Saybrook and Old Lyme. As the river enters the sound, 19,600 feet of water are discharged per second, producing 70 percent of Long Island Sound's fresh water.

The Connecticut River valley was formed as glaciers that covered most of New England receded north about twelve thousand years ago. Lake Hitchcock, one of the largest glacial lakes in North America, extended from Middletown, Connecticut, to Bath, New Hampshire, a distance of 210 miles—a lake slightly larger than Lake Huron. More than half of today's river lies within that basin. Man began to inhabit the fertile ground around the river left behind by the retreating glacier. Artifacts near the town of Gill, Massachusetts, (near Northfield) and East Windsor, Connecticut, show the presence of man from between five thousand and eight thousand years ago. Rock engravings found in Bellows Falls, Vermont, and Claremont, New Hampshire, date the presence of Native Americans to 800 AD. The soil was rich, the woods bounteous with game. The river, filled with fish, served as a highway for nomadic tribes.

It was that richness of the region, made accessible and commercially viable by the river, that attracted settlers. Shipping cargo by water has long had economic advantages over moving goods by land. In a recent interview, the economist Thomas Sowell was quoted: "If you are born up in the mountains and someone else is born in the river valley, then the odds are huge against you of ever being as prosperous as the person born near the river." But, for commerce-focused European settlers, the Connecticut River had to be navigable from its source near the Canadian border to its confluence with the sea. Problems to overcome included rapids, such as the falls in Windsor, Connecticut; South Hadley, Massachusetts; and a number in the Vermont towns of Barnet, Wilder, Hartland, Bellows Falls, and White River Junction. Between 1791 and 1828, a series of transport canals were chartered and constructed, the first in South Hadley and the last in Windsor Locks, Connecticut. The canals facilitated river traffic and by 1848 manufacturers commandeered enough waterpower to operate 450 mills. In Holyoke, where there were no rapids, a dam was constructed to divert water into canals for industrial purposes. In those early industrial days, the United States economically was a "third-world" country, where commerce took precedence over the environment.

But as we grew wealthier, attitudes changed, albeit slowly. There remain more than a thousand active and remnant dams in the four-state Connecticut River watershed, but only fifteen—including two that are breached—on the Connecticut. Four of those are in Pittsburg, New Hampshire, including the Murphy Dam, which is 106 feet high. Eight of the dams are used to produce electricity. While commerce on the river served to help transform an agrarian society into an industrial one, the environmental damage done was not addressed until the 1950s, beginning with the construction of fish ladders that allowed some species to bypass dams. It is not just anadromous fish that migrate upstream to spawn; all species of trout and several species of bass migrate from the Connecticut to smaller tributaries, to find the right habitat for successful spawning. Besides blocking passage, dams cause the temperature of the water behind them to warm. As temperatures rise the level of dissolved oxygen declines, damaging many species. Consequently, over the past decade hundreds of dams in the watershed have been removed. Communities have found, according to David L. Deen, former River Steward for the Connecticut River Watershed Council, that the removal of old dams actually eases flooding conditions, especially during melting ice season, because the river flows more naturally. Dams served a purpose in the industrialization of our nation, but their usefulness has declined. Risks of old dams failing, and the damage they cause to the riverine ecosystem, argues for removing them as the best and safest option.

The wealth of the area, its natural beauty, and its proximity to major urban areas (approximately thirty million people live within one hundred miles of the Connecticut) have attracted artists, writers, and musicians. The Cornish Art Colony, in Cornish, New Hampshire, was established in 1895, centered around sculptor Augustus Saint-Gaudens. It is now the Saint-Gaudens National Historic Site. In its prime it was visited by artists like George de Forest Brush, Maxfield Parrish, and Frederick Remington. The Old Lyme Art Colony (Connecticut) was established in 1899 by Henry Ward Ranger and was instrumental in the development of American Impressionists like Willard Metcalf, Guy C. Wiggins, and Childe

Hassam. Today, the Florence Griswold Museum has recreated the house and the grounds these artists once roamed. From the Marlboro (Vermont) Music Festival to Musical Masterworks in Old Lyme, music has been important to the area. Mark Twain, Harriet Beecher Stowe, and Edith Wharton all lived or spent time at Nook Farm in Hartford. Between 1769 and 1871, some of the country's top universities were founded in the river valley: Dartmouth, Amherst, Mount Holyoke, Smith, the University of Massachusetts, Trinity, and Wesleyan. Boarding schools, like Deerfield, Mount Hermon, and Loomis Chafee line its shore.

In a 1965 documentary, *The Long Tidal River*, Katherine Hepburn said the river had once been described as America's "best landscaped sewer." Much has changed. In 1972, passage of the Clean Water Act regulated the discharge of pollutants into navigable waters. The Silvio O. Conte National Fish and Wildlife Refuge Act was passed in 1991, which resulted in the establishment of the Silvio O. Conte National Fish and Wildlife Refuge in 1997, to "conserve, protect and enhance the abundance and diversity of native plant, fish, and wildlife species and the ecosystems on which they depend throughout the Connecticut River watershed."

In 1993, the Connecticut River was designated as one of the western hemisphere's forty "last great places." Four years later, in 1997, it was listed as one of fourteen federally-designated American Heritage Rivers, and in 2012 it was named a National Blueway by America's Great Outdoors Initiative. Today, with a focus on environmental education, habitat conservation, and the management of public and private lands, the Conte Refuge encompasses thirty-six thousand acres in New Hampshire, Vermont, Massachusetts, and Connecticut. Thousands of additional acres along the river and in the watershed have been preserved in all four states. The estuary of the river has been nominated as a possible site for a National Estuarine Research Reserve (NERR) by the National Oceanic and Atmospheric Administration (NOAA), a division of the United States Department of Commerce.

The river is home to dozens of fish species: the upper Connecticut holds brook, brown, and rainbow trout, and landlocked salmon, while the lower part of the river is home to striped bass, sea lampreys, shad, and shortnose sturgeon. Twelve varieties of mussels can be found. Deer, black bears, foxes, coyotes, and bobcats roam its banks, while muskrats, beavers, and otters make their living in its waters. Hundreds of native and migratory birds, from partridges, bald eagles, great horned owls, osprey, and seagulls to saltmarsh sparrows, sandpipers, American black ducks, and tree swallows call the river and its marshes home. Dozens of tree species line its banks, from northern spruce, to red and sugar maples, to oak and hickory. The most famous tree along the river is (or was) the "Charter Oak" in Hartford. In 1662, Charles II had granted the Connecticut Colony an unusual degree of autonomy. Twenty-five years later, in 1687, his successor James II demanded the Charter back. But instead of returning it, colonists hid the Charter in a large white oak on the property of Wyllys Hyll. That act of defiance is still remembered, and Connecticut is known today as the Charter Oak State.

The commercial history of the Connecticut is multi-industrial. The river served as a highway, first for Native Americans and later for explorers, trappers, and fishermen. As settlers started farms and formed villages and towns, the river became the principal means for transporting produce and industrial goods—tobacco from flatlands in Connecticut, corn and wheat from fields in Massachusetts, dairy products from Vermont, lumber from New Hampshire, and apples and pears from all four states. Merchants traded with the West Indies and fed coastal cities with produce and meat. Great slabs of Vermont marble, Connecticut brownstone, and New Hampshire granite were carried down the river and became building materials in Boston, New York, and Washington. Shipbuilders in the Connecticut towns of Glastonbury, Portland, and Essex were world renowned, building more than four thousand ships in the nineteenth century. Cities like Hartford, Springfield, and Brattleboro sprouted along its shore, built around saw mills, leather factories, and grain mills. Ivory was imported from Africa for the manufacture of piano keys, buttons, and combs, and nutmeg from Indonesia was used in desserts and in drinks like eggnog and mulled wine, giving Connecticut its second nickname, "the Nutmeg State."

In early years, war along the river was constant. Native American tribes fought one another and allied with either the French or the English, depending on which best served their interests. Settlements along the Connecticut River were suspended in the northern territories during King Phillip's, or Metacomet's, War (1675–1678), causing the abandonment of settlements in Deerfield and Northfield for a generation. Twenty-six years later, after settlers had returned, the famous raid on Deerfield took place, in 1704 during Queen Anne's War (1702–1713). The town was attacked by French soldiers and Native Americans from the Abenaki and Pocomtuc tribes, all under the command of Jean-Baptiste Hertel de Rou-ville. Fifty-six villagers were killed, and a hundred taken to Canada as hostages or prisoners. Two years later, sixty were returned. Settlements along the lower part of the river were affected by the French and Indian War (1754–1763). Two unintended consequences of that war were that it served to unite the colonies against a common enemy, and it allowed the colonists to view their soldiers as a volunteer militia rather than a stand-ing army, which would serve them well thirteen years later.

The Connecticut played other roles in our nation's wars. Connecticut was largely unaffected by battles during the Revolutionary War, but the fertile river valley, along with saltworks in East Haven and ironworks in Salisbury, allowed it to be a provider of necessities for an army. Gen-eral George Washington referred to Connecticut as "the provision state," for its beef, salt, flour, and gunpowder, much of which was delivered via the river. In South Glastonbury, alongside the Connecticut River, the Stocking family owned one of New England's four gunpowder factories. Despite an explosion in 1777 that killed her husband, Eunice Stocking continued to produce gunpowder for the army until the war's end in 1783. On June 13, 1776, the warship *Oliver Cromwell*, the first warship of the Revolution and built by Uriah Hayden, was launched in Essex. The ship seized nine British frigates before being captured by three British ships and renamed HMS *Restoration* in June 1779. Also built in Essex was the world's first submersible craft, the *Turtle*, launched in November 1776 and built by David Bushnell.

During the War of 1812, the British blockaded Long Island Sound, essentially shutting down trade and commerce vital to Connecticut's well-being. And then, on an April night in 1814, a British raiding force rowed the six miles up the River to Pettipaug (now Essex) where they torched twenty-seven ships—the greatest naval loss during the war—and the greatest American naval loss until Pearl Harbor. Gideon Welles of Glastonbury, scion of a shipbuilding family, became Abraham Lincoln's Navy Secretary. The Gildersleeve boat works in Portland produced the steam-powered gunboat the *Cayuga* in 1861 and the *United States* in 1864, the largest steamship in the country with a gross register tonnage of 1289. (She was lost off Cape Romain—South Carolina—in 1881.) Sandbars at

The *Spirit of Saint Louis*
In his autobiography, Lindberg mentions crossing
the mouth of the Connecticut River, May 20, 1927.

the mouth of the Connecticut River meant that steam boilers and cannon could only be placed on ships once they had left the river. During the Civil War, the River served as the means of transporting weapon-making machinery from Pratt and Whitney, engines from Woodruff and Beach and weapons from Colt. By war's end, Connecticut arms manufacturers had supplied 43 percent of all rifle muskets, breech-loading rifles, carbines, and revolvers bought by the Union War Department. The motor patrol boat, USS *Dauntless* was built in Essex in 1917 as a private motorboat and then leased by the US Navy during World War I.

On his renowned flight to Paris in May 1927, Charles Lindberg flew over the mouth of the river. In his 1953 book, *The Spirit of St. Louis*, Lindberg wrote of the experience: "As I approach shore, near the Connecticut River's mouth, wing tips tremble again. For some reason it bothers me less than before. Possibly the air isn't as rough. Possibly I feel that the structure passed its crucial test over Long Island. It may be my knowledge that the plane is already a few pounds lighter; or simply optimism springing from a successful start. At any rate, the bumps no longer cause an ache in my armpits." The Connecticut River, its history and magnitude, has earned our respect and deserves our support. That can be as simple as picking up someone else's litter or avoiding a Jack-in-the-Pulpit, or as complex as negotiating a land deal to acquire more open space or constructing ladders for spawning fish. Because of abundant natural resources, such as the Connecticut provides, and an ethic that reveres hard work, we have become, as a nation, wealthy. Americans are a generous people who give back a larger percentage of income and wealth than any other people. The river has long had a need for conservation. In an 1819 publication of *A Statistical Account of Middlesex County*, the author wrote regarding the Connecticut River: "For several years, the quantity of fish in the river has very considerably decreased." Overfishing, raw sewage, residue from tanneries and a lead mine were all, in part, responsible. The Industrial Revolution was in its infancy, and the river became more polluted as living standards were deemed more important than the environment. But as wealth came, attitudes changed, and the river has become cleaner and the environment purer. Today, there are hundreds of non-profits the length of the river helping to conserve its heritage. Is there more to be done? Certainly, but consider where we are today versus a hundred years ago, versus fifty years ago, and twenty years ago.

Those of us who live in towns along this "long tidal river" have the Connecticut River in common. In 1806, Yale president Timothy Dwight visited the Connecticut River Valley on horseback. He wrote: "The inhabitants of this valley . . . possess a common character, and, in all the different states, resemble each other more than their fellow citizens who live on the coasts resemble them." The river is part of our lives. We drive over it on superhighways and cross over it under covered bridges. We take ferries. We use it for sports, kayaking in its northern parts and in saltwater marshes near its mouth. Scullers and oarsmen race on the river in Hanover, New Hampshire; Greenfield and Amherst, Massachusetts; and Hartford and Middletown, Connecticut. We fish its waters—for trout in Pittsburg, New Hampshire, and shad in Essex, Connecticut. We should and we must conserve what we have been gifted. But we must also recognize that part of wisdom is being adaptable—not trying to change nature's natural forces, playing neither Devil nor God. Twenty-six years ago, the essayist and environmentalist Edward Abbey wrote: "I choose to listen to the river for a while, thinking river thoughts, before joining the night and the stars." Good advice, as we give thanks for the Connecticut River—a repository of history, a source of beauty and delight and a treasure to be enjoyed and conserved.

Autumn
November 7, 2020

Every leaf speaks bliss to me,
fluttering from the autumn tree.

"Fall, leaves, fall"
Emily Brontë (1818–1848)

It may be that trees are mostly leafless and that morning windshields must be cleared of frost, but November 7 is just over halfway through the autumn season. It is my favorite time of year, reminding me of Goldilocks' porridge—in summer we walk in the shade to stay cool; in winter we walk in the sun to stay warm—now, the temperature is just right, so we follow our feet wherever they lead.

Fall is for walking, and among the many attractions of Essex Meadows are the trails that meander through its one-hundred acres of fields, meadows, and woods, some of which connect with those in the 1,000-acre Preserve, providing miles on which to meander or hike.

Normally, Caroline and I go together, hand-in-hand, as we did in Boston almost sixty years ago and as we did more recently along Smith Neck Road in Old Lyme. On this October day, I went out alone. I crossed the drive and onto the golf course. Near the second pin stands a small sugar maple, which was decked out in yellow. Just west was a red maple offering contrast. Squirrels scurried about, cheeks stuffed with nuts and berries. As I walked behind the garages to the back part of the golf course, a few wintering birds made their presence known—probably white-throated sparrows, but not being an ornithologist, I was not sure. A hawk (possibly a sharp-shinned hawk) circled over the mowed grass, looking for mice.

My walk took me through woods, across the back meadow, the one with bent birches, where I picked up a walking stick left a day earlier. The trail rises gently toward the cascade—a grand name for an eight-foot drop and a trickle of water! The trail had been swept of dead leaves, exposing roots, thus making walking safer and easier. At the cascade, I followed the Blue Dot trail south and west, crossed the access road, and made my way to the top of the hill where the powerline cuts through. The woods at this

Autumn colors in Essex

time of year are lovely and being alone gives one the opportunity to think and be thankful for all we have. I am not alone in this feeling of wonder. Quoting a recent Norway study, Teja Pattabhiraman wrote in *The Epoch Times* that "seeking awe from the splendor of nature can give an outdoor walk even more healthful effects. . . . When people are primed to experience awe, they feel simultaneously smaller and better."

Returning down the access road, I left my walking stick camouflaged against a small tree. As I walked through the meadow just beyond the garden, a garter snake slithered out of my way—more startled, I am sure, than was I. Crossing the little stream that becomes the Mud River, I stopped to look down, marveling at the number of creatures that make this place home. That rivulet flows through our swamp—one of our treasures—before making its way into the Fall River, thence to the Connecticut and then to the sea.

In the fall, much of nature, like some of our neighbors, pack for the winter. Much of plant life retires into the ground; insects and small organisms prepare for the cold. Turtles and frogs bury into the muck. Small mammals prepare to hibernate. I head home to a hot chocolate!

Sitting by our electric fireplace, I nurse my hot chocolate, thankful to be alive in this season, to live in New England and especially in Connecticut, with its autumn offerings that soothe and affirm life.

Musings on Nature and Literature
February 10, 2021

No animal, according to the rules of animal etiquette is ever expected to do anything strenuous, or heroic, or even moderately active during the off-season of winter.

Kenneth Grahame (1859–1932)
The Wind in the Willows, 1908

The rubric above describes Rat, Mole, and Badger discussing the most recent smashup of Mr. Toad in his automobile. He was their friend, after all, and shouldn't friends do something? But it was winter and, as Mr. Grahame wrote, most animals "are weather-bound, more or less; and all are resting from arduous days and nights. . . ."

Of course, not all animals sleep through the winter, or hibernate as the more sophisticated among us would say. And, of course, birds who spend winters in Connecticut must survive harsh winter storms and periods of below freezing temperatures—not easy for creatures whose body temperatures run about 105 degrees Fahrenheit and who must consume between a quarter and a half of their body weight every day. Of course, living within a feathered coat has advantages, but still. . . . A dozen and more birds spend the winters near where we live, including house finches, house sparrows, tufted titmice, black-capped chickadees, and at least one pileated woodpecker.

I was delighted to finally see our pileated woodpecker one morning, dining on carpenter ants on a leafless tree in a swampy area of the Mud River where a beaver has been harvesting timber. He was beautiful to see. With a body the size of a crow, he was elegantly dressed in a black tuxedo, with white tie and a distinctive red crown, looking like New York's Cardinal Timothy Dolan, dressed in a black cassock, wearing his red biretta.

Still, I worried about the effects of cold weather. The woodpecker wore no scarf, mittens, or galoshes. I don't believe his meal was warmed in an oven or accompanied with a hot toddy. A tendency to anthropomorphize animals dates to my childhood. While I take joy in assigning human traits to the wildlife, there are those who do not. Patricia Ganea, assistant professor of applied psychology and human development at the

University of Toronto, is one. In an interview with her college newspaper, she said, ". . . children who have more direct experience with real animals in their daily life may be less influenced in their reasoning by anthropocentric portrayals of animals in books." I grew up with animals—horses, goats, and chickens, along with the usual assortment of dogs and cats. But I also grew up on a diet of Aesop's *Fables*, Beatrix Potter, Thornton W. Burgess, Kenneth Grahame, Hugh Lofting, A. A. Milne, Lewis Carroll, E. B. White, and others. I benefitted from real animals, as well as from children's literature. I have never forgotten Peter Rabbit, Mrs. Bluebird, Toad, Jip, Pooh, the White Rabbit, Charlotte, or Stuart Little.

As an adult, I read Tolkien's *Lord of the Rings*, C. S. Lewis's *Chronicles of Narnia*, and returned to Lewis Carroll's *Alice in Wonderland*. With my grandchildren, I read J. K. Rowling's Harry Potter series. In each, besides the pleasure of reading, the purpose is to instruct—to make moral judgments like learning right from wrong; to appreciate the rewards of hard work and personal responsibility; to understand the value of kindness; and to help overcome fear. We are horrified by Gollum and dazzled with talking trees, impressed with Bree and inspired by Aslan, cheered by Humpty Dumpty and amused by the Cheshire Cat, and come to understand the wisdom of Hedwig. A reading of George Orwell's *Animal Farm* teaches that a revolution may replace an autocrat (the human, Farmer Jones) with a worse dictator (the pig, Napoleon). History is filled with

"Mr. Toad"

lessons learned from animals. For example, take Robert the Bruce, King of the Scots and defeated six times by the English: Alone in a cave, he watched a spider try to spin her web. Only on her seventh attempt did she succeed. The moral: no matter how hopeless a situation may seem, never give up. Bruce did not; he left the cave and defeated Edward II at the Battle of Bannockburn in June 1314.

Animals, both real and imagined, have been part of our fifty-seven-year marriage. We have owned, at some point, one pony, two horses, four goats (one of whom gave birth!), four sheep, a number of pigs, and, of course, dogs and cats. With the exception of the pigs, which were raised to be slaughtered, all were given names—the first step toward anthropomorphizing our four-legged friends. Today we have no animals, but our shelves are filled with books of talking animals, many from our childhoods. And when walking through the woods, we look for those who watch every move we make. Assigning them human traits fuels our imaginations and provides empathy. The chipmunk represents youth as it scurries about; in the deer we observe beauty and grace; the muskrat, as he swims home, reflects domesticity; a silent snapping turtle is endowed with the wisdom age brings. And the pileated woodpecker constitutes common sense, as he concentrates on dinner. In her interview, Professor Ganea added: "Books that portray animals realistically lead to more learning and more accurate biological understanding." I wonder?

Perhaps she is right, but I believe she is the one missing out. True, there are lessons to be learned of a scientific nature, as we walk through our hundred-acre wood: How life evolved over millions of years. We see trees that have stood for a hundred years and more. We note the symbiosis between plant to animal and animal to animal that seems miraculous yet is natural. We observe the adaptability of plants and animals, which Peter Wohlleben described so well in his books *The Hidden Life of Trees* and *The Inner Life of Animals*. But there are also lessons to be learned in using one's imagination and seeing animals and even plants as sentient beings.

Dr. Doolittle was a physician who preferred animal patients to humans. He learned their languages, which provided him better understanding. The character was created by Hugh Lofting during the First World War, so one might argue his stories are escapist. Perhaps, but I believe he wanted us to view animals as capable of having feelings—the affection of a mother for her young, the sense of loss when a parent or child

dies, territorial rights, a realization of pain and suffering. Would knowing the Latin name for the pileated woodpecker add to my appreciation
as he hunts for food on a cold winter's morn? I don't think so. Professor
Ganea may find me lazy and a dilletante, but that's okay.

So, during these long winter months, I worry about Mr. Toad and
empathize with Rat, Mole, and Badger. Sitting in my easy chair, sipping
hot cocoa, I look out on the stream, swamp, fields, and woods where my
hibernating friends rest up for the arrival of another spring, and I marvel
at their ability to survive without a book from the Toadstool Bookshop,
a sweater from L. L. Bean, or a hot cup of cocoa.

Spring's Return
March 20, 2021

Spring work is going on with joyful enthusiasm.

John Muir
The Wilderness World of John Muir, 1954
Edited by Edwin Way Teale

In Frances Hodgson Burnett's 1911 novel, *The Secret Garden*, twelve-year-old Colin Craven, who has been bedridden with a spinal injury, looks up from his wheelchair: " 'Is the spring coming?' he asked. 'What is it like?' 'It is the sun shining on the rain and rain falling on the sunshine,' " answers his twelve-year-old cousin Mary Lennox. In *Anna Karenina*, Leo Tolstoy, wrote, "Spring is the time of plans and projects"—a message heeded by gardeners everywhere. Spring carries us from March winds, through April's rains, to May's buds and June's flowers—from seeded furrows to blossoming borders. In the northern hemisphere, the vernal equinox is today, when the sun, on its northward journey, crosses the celestial equator.

In early spring, weather is uncertain. When I was growing up, a New Hampshire slogan proclaimed March skiing to be the season's best. A favorite memory is skiing shirtless on a warm afternoon in late March—getting high on sun and snow. Freezing nights and warm days mean sugar maple sap is running, providing one of nature's most delicious products. Changing temperatures are endemic to spring. At the New England Society's annual dinner in New York on December 22, 1876, Mark Twain spoke: "In the spring I have counted one hundred and thirty-six different kinds of weather inside of four-and-twenty hours." For us, it is common to see temperatures vary by thirty degrees and more in a day.

It is spring's return, its promise of rebirth, from cold winters to warm summers, that makes the season, like Christ's resurrection, seem magical. Yet it is real, and its progress is inexorable. E. B. White, in *Points of My Compass*, wrote, "No matter what changes take place in the world, or in me, nothing ever seems to disturb the face of spring." Following the five-day battle for Mount Belvedere in Italy's Northern Apennines, in which 213 soldiers of the 10th Mountain Division were killed, my father wrote

[64]

to my mother. Instead of death, he wrote of life: "There were crocuses in bloom on Mount Belvedere and the view was beautiful, both day and night, a strange setting for a battle." In Tolkien's *The Return of the King*, it was the end of winter when Frodo Baggins, accompanied by Sam Gamgee, returned to the Shire, after seventeen years of war: "Do you remember the Shire, Mr. Frodo? It'll be spring soon. And the orchards will be in blossom. And the birds will be nesting in the hazel thicket. And they'll be sowing the summer barley in the lower fields . . . and eating the first of the strawberries with cream. Do you remember the taste of strawberries?" I do. I remember picking strawberries in June, in a field next to the abandoned "Brick House," about a half mile from our home. They hid their red faces beneath green leaves, but when found their taste, mingled with the odor of fresh meadow grass, was sweeter than anything store-bought.

Springtime is for lovers, and it is not just for humans. All animal and plant life heed nature's call. A quote attributed to Sitting Bull is a reminder of love's universality: "Behold my friends, the spring is come; the

Eastern box turtle

earth has gladly received the embraces of the sun, and we shall soon see the results of their love." Wakened from long winter nights, hibernating animals exit lairs, searching for a mate. Trees bud, and spring flowers test the air. Peepers chirp, squirrels fluff their tails, and songbirds sing, while black snakes and turtles silently reappear, smiling prettily, seeking sunlight, ready to couple.

But it is the love of two people that poets and playwrights celebrate: "In the spring a young man's fancy lightly turns to thoughts of love," wrote Alfred Lord Tennyson in "Locksley Hall." Proteus speaks in Act I of Shakespeare's *Two Gentlemen from Verona*:

> *O, how this spring of love resembleth*
> *The uncertain glory of an April day,*
> *Which now shows all the beauty of the sun,*
> *And by and by a cloud takes all away."*

The cloud dissipates; he and Julia wed. As did Caroline and I, on an April afternoon in 1964.

Perhaps it is age, but Toby Keith's song, "Don't Let the Old Man In," strikes a chord: "Don't let the old man in; get up and go outside." Keeping the old man at a distance, we do go outdoors. The air is fresh and cool. As my wife and I walk past a pond where a beaver has been busy, across the golf course and on trails through woods and fields, life stirs. Returning birds occupy old nests or build new ones. Hawks circle, looking for field mice blinded by the sunlight. Eight days ago, we saw our first frog of the year and then our first turtle and heard our first peepers. I was reminded of when my mother would offer a nickel to the first of her children to see a turtle each spring. I put out my hand, but she wasn't there.

Nevertheless, I rejoice at spring's return.

Charlotte Williams Neinas
July 2, 1946–December 1, 2020

*You must learn some of my philosophy. Think only of
the past as its remembrance gives you pleasure.*

Jane Austen (1775–1817)
Pride and Prejudice, 1813
Elizabeth Bennet speaking to Darcy

Life is not fair. Was it fair to have been born a slave on a Mississippi cotton plantation in 1830, or to be born Jewish in Europe in the decades before the rise of Nazism in Germany? Why are some born tall and slim and others short and stocky. Some are born with athletic ability, others with poor coordination. Some are naturally talented, in the arts, music, or dance. Others struggle to draw a straight line, carry a tune, or avoid stepping on a partner's toes. Some are accident-prone, while others skip through life with nary a bruise. Why? Some like my brother, Stuart, are born with life-limiting conditions, in his case, a rare genetic disorder called Prader-Willi. Others, like my father and sister, Mary, develop cancer, and die too young. And some, like Charlotte, are afflicted with Alzheimer's, a disease of the brain that causes the individual to forget and lose the ability to think. Why her and not me? Why is life unfair?

Why are some of us saved from such calamities and others, despite living healthy, constructive lives, destined for tragedy? These are questions without answers. We are born and must make the most of the lives and time we are given. We live in an age of data and science—follow the science, we are told—yet there remains much that is mysterious, where answers are sought in other realms. We can look back—and we should, with a smile when we can—but the future is unknowable. Our destinies are not predetermined, at least not in any known way; we have no foreknowledge of what lies ahead.

Charlotte (the middle child of nine), married to David Sobe, bore two children, Noah and Liz, and was grandmother to four—Amelia, Philomena, Maisie, and Charlie. Divorced, she later found in Fred Neinas a loving partner and husband. "Charlotte is," Fred told Caroline and me three

Charlotte

years ago, "my soul mate." Seeing them together, it was obvious the great love they shared, even after her mind had begun to fade.

Growing up in large families, children divide into cohorts: In my case, the three oldest—my older sister, Mary, younger brother, Frank, and I were one. Betsy, Charlotte, and Jenny were a second, and the three younger boys, Stuart, Willard, and George, a third. Charlotte had just turned ten when I went off to boarding school. As a consequence, I only got to know her later.

Nevertheless, memories flood back: It is around 1951. Charlotte is four, about to turn five. I am ten. We have been playing in the hayloft, when Charlotte falls through the trap door, about seven feet to the wooden floor below. She is moaning, not really crying, so I carry her back to the house. She is whisked off to the doctor who determines she suffered a concussion.

On winter weekends, we skate on Fly Pond and ski at Whit's Tow. We start on the beginners' slope, where I picture Charlotte aged five or six. Us older (and not necessarily responsible) children have to periodically check on the younger ones. If cold, we might share a hot chocolate, served by Mrs. Whitcomb. In summers, we swim in Hancock's Norway Pond, and we ride horseback. I ride "Judy," a cross between a workhorse and a thoroughbred. Charlotte is on "Mitzi," an aging Shetland pony. When "Mitzi" starts off first, she will not let "Judy" pass, causing me to use language not allowed at home.

Years pass. Charlotte grows up and meets David at the University of New Hampshire. They fall in love and become engaged in 1968. In that same year, our father develops cancer and dies on December 2. Charlotte and David are married the following July, and it falls to me, as the oldest son, to give her away—a strange feeling for a twenty-eight-year-old who, like his sister, is still feeling the loss of our father. For the first year, they live in Canton, Connecticut, about thirty-five miles from where we live in Durham, so Caroline and I, with our, then, two young children, visit.

Later, Charlotte and David move to Peterborough and build a house on land adjacent to our mother's. Charlotte has a successful career as a development officer, first at the Dublin School in Dublin, New Hampshire, which her children attend, and later at Wheelock College and Suffolk University, both in Boston.

❧

Sometime in the 1990s, we decided on a family ski weekend at Mount Sunapee, about thirty-five miles west and north of Concord, New Hampshire.

It is a place where our father would take us when Whit's Ski Tow grew too small. So, we all had fond memories, which brought us into orbit with re-membrances of our father who had died a quarter century earlier. Charlotte and Fred, then living in Cambridge, and I would spend the weekend at Rosewood Country Inn in Bradford, a small comfortable place with a great breakfast. For dinner we would go to the Colby Hill Inn in Henniker or the Inn at Pleasant Lake in New London. While we skied all day with other family members—siblings, in-laws, children, nieces, and nephews—the three of us would spend the evenings together. Over the years, I saw more of Charlotte during those two or three days than at any point since we were children. The twinkle in her eye and her laughter, which was contagious, made merry those days and evenings, memories I cherish.

And, sadly, it was also at Rosewood Inn that I first noticed a change in Charlotte. Fred and I were alone, putting skis in the car. I asked him about what seemed to be her repetitious questions. He told me doctors had confirmed an early onset of Alzheimer's. A few months later, Fred arranged a move to the Taylor community in Laconia, New Hampshire, where he had practiced medicine and where his two daughters lived. He told Charlotte the move was necessary because he was older, and he did not want her to be alone should something happen to him. For a year and a half, they lived in their cottage, until it was time for Charlotte to move to the memory unit, the most difficult decision Fred ever made.

The rest of the story you can imagine, but as Elizabeth Bennet says to Darcy, and as Charlotte lived her life, we should savor those memories that give us pleasure—memories that make one's eyes twinkle and hearts joyful. It is what Charlotte would want.

MEMORIES

The fifteen essays in this section include stories of growing up in the 1940s and 1950s. There is an essay on Christmases remembered and of its association—sometimes forgotten in this age of materialism, relativism, and inclusion—with Christianity. There is another simply focusing on Christmases past, and one on the remembrance of a wonderful friend who died just two months shy of his one-hundredth birthday. And there is one, "The Home Stretch," which equates our lives with a horse race. The common theme is one of remembrance.

∾

Christmas and Christianity
December 21, 2015

"Maybe Christmas," the Grinch thought, "doesn't come from a store."

Theodor (Dr. Seuss) Geisel (1904–1991)
How the Grinch Stole Christmas, 1957

Christmas is special—perhaps the most special of all holidays, at least for children. In its pervasiveness, it has become ecumenical. It is as much a feeling as a season. Could the spontaneous truce that for a few moments interrupted fighting in the trenches on the Western Front in December 1914 have occurred at any time other than Christmas Eve? It is a magical time. The power to believe is granted to those whose faith runs deep but inherent in all children. To them, Santa Claus is not an abstraction; he is real. When Theodore Roosevelt, in the interest of conservation, announced that the White House would go without a Christmas tree in 1902, he was denied by his two youngest sons, Archibald and Quentin. "Scrooge" and "Tiny Tim" taught us the ugliness of greed and the grace of benevolence.

Growing up in rural New Hampshire, Christmases were special. On its Eve my father would hitch "Judy" to a sledge. We children would climb aboard. With dogs following eagerly, we headed through the gate leading to the "next field" and the rutted road beyond, into the woods. A previously located spruce or fir would be cut down, placed aboard the sledge, and returned to the house. That evening my parents would decorate it, the best part being when real candles, scattered among its still-damp branches, were lit—a bucket of water placed prudently nearby. We would then hang up our stockings. "Mitzi," our Shetland, would come into the living room and hang up her "shoe." Later, we would gather around our mother, as she read: "'Twas the night before Christmas. . . ."

Neither of my parents were religious in a traditional sense. My mother had been raised in New Haven as a Congregationalist, my father as a Unitarian in Wellesley. There was a time in the 1950s when my father attended church regularly, which was due to his fondness for the minister, David B. Parke. Caroline and I raised our children in the Episcopal

Grandson Alex's train set, which he built

faith, the church in which my wife was baptized. When our children were young, we attended services regularly. In fact, at one point I was a member of the vestry, and our children were acolytes. But as we grew older, we became irregular communicants. Nevertheless, I take comfort in a familiarity with the liturgy and hymns. I enjoy the wisdom of our rector, revealed in his sermons. And I love the pageantry of Christmas services.

While the commercialization of Christmas is a reality, it remains a religious holiday. There are about 2.3 billion Christians in the world—the most of any religion on the planet. According to PEW Research, 71 percent of Americans identify as Christian. There was a time, however, when intolerance was essentially synonymous with Christianity. Consider: The Crusades—the first began in 1095 and the last in 1248; there was a time when popes led armies—Pope Julius II (1443–1513), one of the last to lead an army, named himself after Julius Caesar; there was the Spanish Inquisition, which began in 1478 and disbanded in 1834. Think of Puritans in New England who, in seventeenth-century Salem, hung Sarah Good and eighteen other women for witchcraft; and remember the fictional Hester Prynne, ostracized for adultery. But that era passed. Nineteenth- and twentieth-century Christian missionaries may have been exuberant in spreading the Gospel, but they did so peacefully. They were more likely to be killed than to kill.

One of the most profound changes in the global religious landscape has been the decline of Christianity in the region of its birth—the Middle East. By 2010, the percent of the population that was Christian had declined by two-thirds from a hundred years earlier. In the past five years, in Iraq and Syria, the number of Christians has declined by 60 to 75 percent. "Religious cleansing," a euphemism for genocide, is being practiced on Christians in ISIS-controlled territories in Syria, Iraq, and sub-Saharan Africa. In our homes, keeping warm before blazing yule logs as we prepare to celebrate Christmas, it is hard to imagine (but we should not forget) that Christians are still being killed—some crucified—simply for being Christian.

The word "Christmas" stems from the old English *Cristes Moesse*. It means a celebration of the Eucharist in honor of the Messiah, or Christ—Jesus the Christ. Today we celebrate the holiday as the time of His birth, in a stable in Bethlehem. That city now has a population of 25,000. Bethlehem is located five miles south of Jerusalem in the West Bank. Roughly 55 percent of the population is Muslim, with the bulk of the rest being Christian.

In most families, Christmas is a cherished tradition. It provides children a sense of place—something to look forward to each year. For adults, it brings back memories of childhood, of the way holidays were once celebrated. But there is nothing wrong with developing new customs or amending old ones. My children were raised differently than I. It is likely that, as they marry and have children, their children will develop their own traditions. Change can be good and is, in fact, necessary. In "The Custom House," the introductory chapter that sets the stage for *The Scarlet Letter*, Nathaniel Hawthorne wrote: "Human nature will not flourish, any more than a potato, if it be planted and replanted, in the same worn-out soil." His words speak to the pluralism of America's society. They remind us that immigrants who come to America, over time, affect our culture. They integrate and form our unique American culture.

During this season it is worth reminding ourselves that the word "holiday" also has religious antecedents. The word is derived from the Old English, *haligdaeg,* meaning "holy day." In that spirit, I wish you joy, peace, goodwill, and good health. Caroline and I will spend Christmas with our family—our three children, their spouses, and our ten grandchildren. The magic of Christmas still exists for my youngest grandchildren. And even for the older ones, who are hesitant to deny the existence of Santa Claus . . . just in case.

Whatever your religion or whatever code you live by, may it bring peace and good cheer to you and to all you encounter. The Grinch was right. Christmas does not come from the store. It comes from the heart.

Road Trip
February 2, 2017

Alice: "Would you tell me please, which way I ought to go from here?"
"That depends on where you want to go," said the Cat.
"I don't much care where," said Alice.
"Then it doesn't matter which way you go," said the Cat.

Lewis Carroll (1832–1898)
Alice's Adventures in Wonderland, 1867

. . .not all those who wander are lost.

J. R. R. Tolkien (1892–1973)
Gandalf to Frodo in *The Fellowship of the Ring,* 1954

Twenty-five years ago, my wife and I joined a club in Florida, twenty miles north of Fort Lauderdale. We have flown down to visit it during the winter every year since. This year we decided to drive.

When I was first in college, road trips were common. Guys (mostly) would jump into a car and head out, usually with girls and beer in mind—not always in that order. Once, when I was twenty, I drove alone and without stopping, other than for gas, the 710 miles from Sudbury, Ontario, to Greenwich, Connecticut. The trip took eighteen hours. Exhausting; not to be repeated.

My favorite auto trip was through Europe with my wife in the winter–spring of 1965. My erratic college career ended that February with my having completed courses for a degree. A job with Eastman Kodak would start in June. We had been married a year earlier in April. During my last two years in college, I had held multiple jobs—driving a school bus, working in a sandwich shop, selling $2.00-win tickets at Rockingham State Park, and writing a sports column for *Foster's Daily Democrat.* I was also an Army reservist. Caroline typed a tedious manuscript for a professor. With rent of $85.00 a month, no telephone, and $15.00 a week allotted for groceries, we saved $2,000. We bought round-trip tickets to Paris, rented a Volkswagen bug, and, with Arthur Frommer's *Europe on $5 a Day* tucked under our arms, spent eleven glorious weeks touring southern Europe.

Road trips have a long history, dating back long before cars. Two of the most famous fictional heroic trips were ones by Odysseus and Lemuel Gulliver. According to Homer's epic poem, Odysseus took ten years to return from Troy (located not far from Gallipoli) where he had waged war for ten years. The story tracks the adventures he encountered, as he traveled the 670 miles back to Ithaca and his patient wife Penelope. Jonathon Swift's Gulliver sailed to the South Seas and beyond. He left England in 1699 and did not return until 1715. Thousands of writers have since described the pull of the open road and the romance of the unknown. In *Travels with Charley*, John Steinbeck drove the 10,000-mile perimeter of the country with his poodle. He wrote: "I am happy to report that in the war between reality and romance, reality is not the stronger." Three years earlier, in 1957, Jack Kerouac, wrote his best-known novel, *On the Road*. On the road, in his case, was more of a sociological trip into the counter-cultural world of the "Beat" generation, with its jazz, poetry, and drugs.

Hollywood has long used road trips to entertain viewers and score box office successes. Think of all the *On the Road to . . .* movies with Bing Crosby and Bob Hope. Viewers were transported to Rio, Singapore, Zanzibar, Morocco, and more. Consider the darkness of Ida Lupino's *The Hitch-Hiker*, a movie produced in 1953, starring Edmond O'Brien; Peter Fonda's *Easy Rider*, produced in 1969, starring himself and Dennis Hopper; *Five Easy Pieces*, with Jack Nicholson and Karen Black (a movie which includes my favorite line about ordering buttered toast); the slap-stick humor of Chevy Chase in 1983's *National Lampoon's Vacation*; or Susan Sarandon and Geena Davis in *Thelma & Louise*.

But our trip to Florida would be different, tamer, more choreographed. We expected to be neither gone for years like Odysseus, nor tied up by Lilliputians like Gulliver. We weren't going to pick up hitchhikers or search for the meaning of life. We had one another for company, not a dog and certainly no strangers. In contrast to Kerouac, we are not counter-culturalists. Unlike our honeymoon fifty-two years ago, there would be no sleeping bags, or living on $5.00 a day. We planned where we would be every night. And, unlike my drive down from Canada, no day would involve a distance of more than 400 miles, and we would not drive after dark.

We left Essex on January 1, after celebrating our grandson George's twelfth birthday in Lyme, and drove the eighty miles to our daughter's home in Rye. A happy omen was leaving one happy household for another. The next day we drove to Richmond, once capital of the Confederacy, a city laced with history. I could not but help think that a drive that took us six hours would have taken a Revolutionary War-era messenger, changing horses every ten miles or so, at least two days to travel that distance, and then only if the horses were fresh and ready to go and the rider didn't sleep. Before the advent of the railroad or cars, it was a two-week trip. We thought of years-ago car trips, when we had to travel through the center of Baltimore and Washington. Now, we just let the navigation system guide us to our hotel. Will self-driving cars be here for our grandchildren, when they, at our age now, make similar trips? Probably. Just enter their destination, sit back, and enjoy the ride. But will they miss the sense of independence that control of a vehicle provides? Will they be able to spontaneously make side trips, or alter their destination?

From Richmond, we drove south, across swamps, down straight, uncongested highways, through the pine barrens of the Carolinas to Savannah where we spent two nights. It is a city neither of us had seen, and we needed a break. We could not help thinking that this onetime home to Forrest Gump was Sherman's goal when he left Atlanta in November 1864 on his "march to the sea." Today it is America's fourth busiest port, with an historic district that combines the beauty of southern architecture with the graciousness of its people, and it serves food so good that, as one guide told us, ". . . there ain't no size six dresses in Savannah!"

From Savannah it was a short hop to Ponte Verde Beach, not far across the border in Florida. Here we bunked with friends from New Jersey who escape the snow and ice every winter for four months in the sun. The following day we drove the long eastern shore of Florida, across marshes, down the flatness of Florida's I-95. While it was the least interesting part of the trip, our destination was in sight.

Nine days later we started home, this time taking twice as long as we had going south. Perhaps it was an instinctive desire to delay getting back to the cold, snow, and wind? On the first day we drove all of forty miles to Wellington, where my youngest brother George lives. Horses had been a part of our life growing up, and George has made a career involving them. He is a Grand Prix rider, president of the United States Dressage Federation, and was recently appointed the only American on the Fédération Equestre Internationale (FEI) Dressage Committee. The following day we headed back to our friends in Ponte Verde Beach, and on the next made a long drive west across the Florida/Georgia border, through conifer and deciduous forests, to LaGrange, Georgia, to visit friends. LaGrange is only seventeen miles from the Alabama border and about seventy miles south and west of Atlanta. It sits in the middle of what was once Georgia's cotton country. The final leg of that drive was through miles of peach orchards—a beautiful part of the world, a place neither of us had seen. The next day we headed back to the coast, to elegant Charleston, where friends welcomed us to the house that they had rented for four months.

After two days in Charleston—one morning spent at Middleton Place, a former rice plantation where the paddies take the form of butterflies—we headed to Petersburg, Virginia, where my great-grandmother, Mary Bolling Kemp, lived during the siege that preceded the end of the Civil War. She was born in Gloucester County on the York River but was in Petersburg as a young child during the siege. I have a photograph of me on her lap a year or so before she died in 1946—a personal link that adds to the meaning of history. From Petersburg we drove the eighty miles to Fredericksburg, scene of one of the Confederacy's famous victories and where Caroline's nephew now lives. The next day we drove to Red Bank, New Jersey, near Rumson, where we have rented a house for the month of August for almost forty years. It is where my wife spent her summers growing up. The next morning we drove back to Rye, to our daughter's, with a carload of laundry, and happy to be back among family. Two days later, rested and with clean clothes, we headed to Essex.

What I missed most in spending days driving was reading the papers. The decline in print media has become increasingly apparent. While I have all the means of getting my news electronically, I prefer the rustle of paper, the ability to turn pages, and the sight of an article I had not considered. So, we listened to news on Sirius radio, but more often than not tuned to "'50s on 5." In the evenings, after a drink and a good dinner, the adventures of Dickens's Little Nell beckoned.

A long trip makes one think about myriad subjects—about our country and the people who populate it—our differences and similarities. We grow accustomed to the people and the geography that surround us. The country is large and there is much we have not seen. On business, I was a "flyover," traveling from New York to the West Coast. On this trip we went to new places, yet still only saw a narrow swath of America. In researching a new book, *Earning the Rockies,* Robert Kaplan visited parts of America that are remote to those of us who have spent most of our lives on one (or both) of the two coasts. He went to the heartland. Kaplan writes that listening without asking is how one learns people's opinions.

In our own lives, surrounded by like-minded people and with so much of our time spent listening to our own voices, we miss what others are saying. A friend of mine, who lives both in Manhattan and the rural South, recently wrote a letter to her niece, a letter she shared with me. She described those living in her small southern town: ". . . a lot of them see themselves as hardworking, tolerant, and good people. That makes them disbelieve the press. . . . It makes them feel un-listened to and, again, a word I hear often: disrespected." No party or political philosophy has a monopoly on intelligence, righteousness, or tolerance. Kaplan's words about listening should serve as an epiphany to those who care about the divisions that separate us. His message is one we should heed.

But enough moralizing. For most of us, there are only two times when we can take such road trips: when we are young and when our hair has turned grey. My wife and I have been fortunate, in that we were able to take such a trip when we first started out together, and now, after more than fifty years of marriage, we did it again, but differently, more comfortably and less spontaneously. Nevertheless, all trips are adventures. My favorite piece about road trips is the last paragraph in E. B. White's novel *Stuart Little,* because it suggests the mystery of the unknown and the start of an adventure: "Stuart rose from the ditch, climbed into his car, and started up the road that led to the north. The sun was just coming up over the hills on his right. As he peered into the great land that stretched before him, the way seemed long. But the sky was bright, and he somehow felt he was headed in the right direction."

As we pulled into the drive, 3,400 miles and twenty-five days after we had left, our adventure was over. We were home, determined to do it again next year.

Growing Up in the 1940s and 1950s
November 20, 2018

Anyway, the consequence of all this is that kids were left pretty much to decide for themselves what games they would play—indeed even to invent their own games.

Antonin Scalia (1936–2016)
Scalia Speaks: Reflections on Law, Faith, and Life Well Lived, 2017

My wife and I spent a few days, recently, at the home of four grand-children, while their parents went to New York for a well-deserved weekend away. While they were at a casino charity gala at the Yale Club, sitting in the bleachers at a Dartmouth–Columbia football game and attending Puccini's *La Fanciulla del West*, with the German tenor Jonas Kaufman, at the Met, we were in our cars. During the roughly forty hours we were at their house, I made fifteen four-mile trips into town. (My wife made a few of her own.) Two of the trips were for my own purposes—buying newspapers—but the rest involved the grandchildren: visits to friends, sporting events, shopping, restaurants, etc. Heading out on the fifteenth trip to somewhere, I thought of the gap between their growing up and mine. My childhood and adolescence took place in the post-Depression and postwar years. My parents, being artists, worked from home. Both of them had traveled abroad when young, but once settled in Peterborough, New Hampshire—apart from the war, visiting parents in East River, Connecticut, and Wellesley, Massachusetts, attending horseshows, and going skiing—they rarely left home. The decades since my childhood have seen vast changes.

In the late 1940s and early 1950s there were, at least in our house, no electronic gadgets apart from a radio on which we listened to Red Sox games on WBZ and shows like *The Lone Ranger, Fibber McGee and Molly,* and *The Shadow.* There were no electric appliances—no stove, refrigerator, washing machine, or dishwasher. There was no blender, TV, or toaster. A woodstove served the house until after I was married—and an electric refrigerator only arrived in 1953. Before that, we made weekly trips to the ice-man. (In my earliest memories ice was delivered, but that service was suspended not long after the War.) Ice was stored in a wooden, tin-lined ice chest and replaced every four or five days. After my father died in 1968, my

My mother with Frank, me, and Mary on "Mitzi"

mother purchased a television and an electric stove. In terms of news, and apart from the radio, my parents subscribed to *The New York Herald Tribune* and *The Peterborough Transcript*. *Life* allowed us to imagine ourselves in foreign and exotic places. We read *The Saturday Evening Post* for its serialized stories and glanced through *The New Yorker* and *Punch* for their cartoons. We read a lot, as there were hundreds of books in the house.

Like many rural families, we had a barn. In our case it housed horses, goats, chickens, a few ducks and, later, a couple of peacocks. The goats were used for milk and butter. The chickens and ducks for eggs. The peacocks for ornamentation. The horses, like the peacocks, were an expense, until my mother began giving riding lessons in the mid-1950s. We usually had five or six horses: "Nona" was a chestnut that had belonged to my father's family; "Jill," a dark-colored horse who, when she died, my father buried in front of the barn. "Judy" was a chestnut cross between a thoroughbred and a workhorse and my usual mount. "Judy" was also used to haul manure and felled trees, which were cut up and split for the woodstoves and fireplace; "Whinny," a grey Welsh pony, was given to my mother by her former headmistress, Miss Charlotte, on the occasion of the birth of her fifth child.

"Star" was sired by an Arabian and foaled by "Whinny," and generally ridden by my brother Frank, and "Mitzi," was the Shetland bought by my mother during the war and on whom we all learned to ride. What I loved best was riding through the woods and over the "hill" to our grandparents' summer home and then galloping home along dirt roads. A favorite pleasure was inviting a friend to go riding, putting him or her on "Mitzi," and then riding past the watering hole, where "Mitzi" would inevitably roll, especially when she sensed an inexperienced rider. Once, at a horse show in Dublin, New Hampshire, I got my foot caught in a stirrup while riding "Whinny" and was dragged about a hundred feet, with no damage except to my ego. But my mother's interest paid off. Her youngest child, George, became nationally ranked as a dressage rider and today is president of the United States Dressage Federation.

We swam and rode horses in the summer, skated and skied in the winter. We played politically incorrect games, like cowboys and Indians, where the youngest were forced to play the Indians, because they always ended up dead. We traipsed through the woods, pretending to be frontiersmen, carrying toy cap guns. (My father did not like guns, so there were never any in the house.) But he did build a jungle gym. It was made from six- to ten-inch diameter trees he had cut down, and it stood about fifteen feet high. It had swings, bars, and crossbeams on which we learned to balance. My sister, Mary, used it as the centerpiece for a Children's Circus, which she organized in the late 1940s and that ran for a dozen years. The proceeds from the Circus—the first generated $30.00—went to the Crotchet Mountain Rehabilitation Center.

We played more humdrum games like marbles, which required a combination of dexterity and guile, with perhaps more emphasis on the latter. We carried them around in little leather pouches. The goal was to win your opponents' marbles. We wrestled, sometimes for fun, other times more seriously. We played catch, and stuck crabapples on the end of a stick to see how far we could catapult them. Once, I broke a dining room window. My mother made me tell my father what I had done. The trip to the studio, where he was working, was a hundred feet from the house. It took hours, or so it seemed. He commended me for my honesty, not knowing credit belonged to my mother. As we got older, and on some weekends, we went to the movies; though I have no memory of my parents ever having gone. An afternoon feature, as I recall, cost twenty-five cents.

Another difference was the cars. My son and his wife, with two children of driving age, own three cars. (An embarrassing admission is that my wife and I, with five drivers in the family, once had six cars.) Until my sister, Mary, and I bought a car together in 1957—a 1947 four-door Ford sedan, for which we paid $95.00—my family had only one car, despite having nine children and living four miles from the village. The first of my parents' cars was a 1938 Chevrolet station wagon. (I have a picture of it on the wall behind my desk, a suitcase tied to its bumper, my sister, Mary, and me in front holding dolls, and a goat sticking her head out the rear window.) Next was a 1941 Ford, bought second-hand after the war. That was followed by a 1953 Ford wagon and, four years later, a 1957 Ford wagon. When my mother hitched the car to the horse trailer to take a few children to a show, my father was out of luck if he needed to go to town. And when my father took a bunch of us skiing, my mother had to stay home.

We took the bus to and from school. After-school activities would not have fit into our parents' lifestyles. "Helicoptering" and "hovering" parents were years in the future. We entertained ourselves. Our nearest neighbor was a mile away. I was the second child, situated between my older sister, Mary, and younger brother, Frank. Next came three girls—Betsy, Charlotte, and Jenny. They were followed by three boys—Stuart, Willard, and George. Essentially, we were trisected, though Mary substituted for everyone's mother when our real mother was in the barn or away. I was less helpful. Chopping wood, pitching hay, and cleaning stalls were chores to be endured, not enjoyed. (I recall once the unpleasant and difficult task of burying a goat who had died when the ground was still frozen.) Most of all, though, we had time to play. Frank and I let our imaginations roam. We played in the woods and fields, sometimes with cap pistols and small hunting knives, the throwing of which was an art we practiced but never mastered. The cap guns, however, were good for scaring chickens, goats, and horses, much to our delight and to their dismay. Sometimes we camped outside, and there were even times when we made it through the night.

Permitting children to travel alone seems quaint in an age when parents have been arrested for letting children walk home from the park or from school. We were warned about speaking to strangers, but "stranger danger" was an alien phrase. I was one of the more outgoing of my siblings, and perhaps that is why my parents let me fly alone when I was thirteen—my first time on a plane. I was to meet my maternal grandmother in the Adirondacks. To get there, I flew from Keene, New Hampshire, to New York's LaGuardia Airport, changed planes, and then on to Lake Placid. I arrived without incident, but with memories that come with the excitement and freedom of being on one's own. Wings began to sprout.

There is no right way of bringing up children, and my fondness for the past does not mean it was better than today. Nevertheless, there were things we did well then and things we can do better today. We should be unafraid of letting children experience failure. We should not confuse sentimentality with compassion. We must recognize differences in children and encourage them in their strengths, while doing our best to correct their weaknesses. Children should be taught the Golden Rule. They should learn civics and the Ten Commandments. Society should encourage the traditional bonds of marriage and acknowledge the benefit of two-parent households, even as we know it is not always possible. We put undue pressure on children today, as their activities are programmed for little or no downtime. Screens take time away from reading; though video games are better than television, as the latter is passive. Luck plays a

1951. Top row: Betsy, Jenny, me
Bottom row: Charlotte, Mary, Stuart, Frank

role. Accidents, without warning, happen. And there are bad people who do bad things. As well, children are different: some mature faster than others; some are better athletes, others more musical or stronger scholastically. Some have disabilities, as did one of my brothers who was born with Prader-Willi syndrome.

But I worry that "safe places" and "trigger warnings" do more harm than good. As much as we would like, we cannot protect children against all harm. They must learn to walk alone, to be independent, and to take responsibility. Government provides invaluable services—a free society could not operate without it. Seventy-five years ago, because of the war, families were disrupted. Single-parent moms struggled to perform both roles. But they knew it was unnatural and, hopefully, temporary—a separation due to the war. The general sense was that government should govern, teachers should teach, and parents should parent.

Back to the rubric at the start of this essay: Justice Scalia grew up about the same time as did I, though our lives were very different. He grew up in the city; I, in the country. His father, a professor of romance languages at Brooklyn College, was an immigrant from Sicily, and his mother, an elementary school teacher, was second-generation Italian. My parents were artists and their families had been here for generations. Justice Scalia was an only child. I was one of nine. He was brilliant and an over-achiever. I was average and an under-achiever. He reached the peak of his profession. I struggled up the rungs of the Wall Street ladder. Nevertheless, we had in common the need to be inventive during our free time as children. His quote, at the top of this essay is from a speech he gave in 1997 at the University Club of Washington, DC. It applies to us both. It was our imaginations that gave currency to our childhoods.

Returning to my grandchildren's driveway for the fifteenth time that weekend, my daydreams evaporated as my mind turned to the job at hand. Don't get me wrong, though, my children and grandchildren are smart, attractive, and entertaining. I love them, and I love being with them.

The Joy of Things
May 16, 2019

*I looked around the rooms I did not see as rooms, but more as landscapes
for my emotions, a biography of memory.*

Anne Spollen
The Shape of Water, 2008

My wife and I have always been collectors, not for investment, but because something struck our fancy: a painting, an old English tea caddy, an antique desk. I have bought old books and Caroline, old china. We have politically incorrect knickknacks, wooden snuff boxes, and cast-iron doorstops. Amidst the books and papers that clutter my built-in desk are two dozen photographs, an old Wall Street cartoon, and the paper ticker, embedded in Lucite, of a trade I helped facilitate many years ago. On the walls of our small library, where seven hundred books have found a home, hang forty-five framed paintings, photographs, drawings, and letters, most having to do with family. Collections, as someone once said or wrote—or should have if they did not—are little more than reflections of the collector. Look at our walls and bookshelves, I tell our grandchildren, and you will learn about us.

The collecting of "things" has become passé, in an age when parents prefer the bustle of in-town living to the placidity of rural life. Collecting can be a selfish avocation, for it is only the self that wants pleasing. Experiences, in contrast, are usually shared. Experiences, of course, are often memorialized in things: photos, mementos, or souvenirs of places and sights visited. But do we take time to savor last year's trip, or are we too busy planning next year's expedition? This is not to argue against experiences, especially with children and grandchildren. God knows I love them, but perspective is wanted, and balance is needed.

Has the pendulum swung too far from "things"? Who, we are asked, would want "brown" furniture in their living room, pieces of junk in the family room, crockery in the pantry, dusty books on shelves, and old paintings on walls? Well, we would. But the furniture is antique and the junk, curios. The crockery is, in fact, Meissen; the "dusty old books" include first editions of *Through the Looking Glass* and *Huckleberry Finn*; and the "old pictures" include a few Connecticut impressionists. While recognizing that changing habits are to be expected, there is a compulsivity toward the "doing of it now" that possesses our ego-obsessed culture, which is troubling, making those like me feel like dinosaurs in the age of Twitter.

Life is more than collecting "things" and even more than experiences. In *The Second Mountain*, David Brooks writes of his climb toward faith: "Happiness comes from accomplishments. Joy comes from offering gifts. Happiness fades; we get used to the things that make us happy. Joy doesn't fade. To live with joy is to live with wonder, gratitude, and hope." There is wisdom in those words. There is so much about the world we do not know and cannot understand. While there are some who claim that all climate change is due to man, I feel humbled when a thunderstorm passes through, a winter storm brings devastation, or the sea churns in enormous, destructive waves. The Atlantic Oceanographic and Meteorological Laboratory tells us that the average hurricane generates and releases energy equivalent to almost two hundred times the electrical generating capacity of the planet. There is no question that man has affected climate, but he is not the only cause. It makes one realize there are forces greater than man. I am filled with wonder of the natural world, gratitude for being alive, and hope for a future that is free and peaceful for my grandchildren.

But is a joyful life simply a belief in God, helping others, or witnessing nature's mysteries? Perhaps. However, in my opinion joy comes from striking the right balance between work, home, play, faith, and community service. Joy stems from being happy with one's self. Certainly, the absence of bad luck plays a role, but it is mostly about walking the line between compulsion and dedication; a willingness to work hard, but not at the expense of ignoring one's family. The Serenity Prayer of Reinhold Niebuhr comes to mind: "God, grant me the serenity to accept the things I cannot change, Courage to change the things I can, and Wisdom to know the difference." When I skied, there was joy in fresh powder on the Bolshoi Ballroom at Vail. Having given up skiing, I find joy in walking through the woods and in putting words on paper. Joy comes from the pleasure of giving back to one's community some of what one has gained. I get joy in our infrequent visits to church. And I get joy in looking at things we have collected over many years—a photograph of me and my sister, each holding dolls, taken around 1943; a painting my wife did while a student in Boston in 1959; a wooden Christmas tree ornament bought in Germany on our honeymoon in 1965; a Henry King Taylor painting, "Carrying Out the Anchor," bought in Haddam, Connecticut, in the late 1960s; a family history discovered at Boston's Goodspeed's in the 1970s; a signed copy of *Midstream* by Helen Keller, and numerous pieces of sculpture and drawings by parents, children, and grandchildren.

It is said that "enough is enough," and that probably applies to this essay. But what does it really mean? Are your demands the same as mine? Life is not (or should not be) a competition. We are here for a moment, and then, like all living things, we die. Are we remembered? Looking at what we have collected, I see history and the memories the objects evoke. A drawing of my father as a child and a silhouette of my mother in her riding habit at age twelve make me think of their childhoods and of how the world has changed. I recall once an aunt coming to our home in Greenwich, seeing a chest that had belonged to her mother, my grandmother. She said how pleased she was to see that piece, well-loved as before, but in its new home. My wife and I feel the same way, seeing things we once owned now gracing rooms or walls in the homes of our children. Each carries a memory; each tells a story, one we relate, and which may (we hope) be passed down to future generations. History is more interesting when personal. "Things" help pave the way.

In defending "things," I am not belittling the experience of a bungee jump in Costa Rica, serving a meal at a soup kitchen, or renewing one's faith. I am suggesting that, in this trip through life, which we are all fortunate to be on, never be embarrassed because you chose a silver cow creamer over a trip to Disney World. It is finding the balance. Self-help books are of little use, as we each wander in different directions. In life it is the trip, not the destination, that is important. David Brooks finds joy in different ways than do I, and what is optimum for me will be different from what is right for you. There is no right or wrong way in the search for joy, only what is most comfortable and what brings peace and comfort, whether it is renewed faith, a sunset on an island beach, or a P. G. Wodehouse first edition.

Remembrances of Christmases Past
November 30, 2019

Christmas is a season, not only of rejoicing but of reflection.

Winston Churchill (1874–1965)

At seventy-eight, the past has consumed most of the time I have been granted—a sobering thought as we approach the most joyous days of the year, the Christmas Season.

Memory is healthy, necessary even. Our minds are remarkable. We tend to remember positive times while relegating bad memories to the dustbin. This is a collection of short recollections of eight Christmases over eight decades, from 1944 to 2012. They speak to the stages of one's life—stages that seemed long when living them, but short on reflection. They mark off one's life in ten-year increments. I marvel at the change a decade can bring, especially when one is young.

Christmas 1944—My earliest memory of Christmas: My father was at Fort Patrick Henry in Virginia, about to be shipped to Italy with the 10th Mountain Division. I knew he was away but paid little attention. My mother had brought us to her parents' home in Madison, Connecticut, when my father entered the army nine months earlier. I was three, about to turn four. My father had been a skier for the past twenty years; he now was with the Ski Troops, so it was thought right to provide me and my sister with skis for Christmas. The small amount of snow on the ground allowed us to try them out. But what I remember best about that Christmas was the red fire engine I received—on which I could sit and, with a wooden handle, turn the front tires, as I wheeled it around the dining room table.

Christmas 1952—By now the war was over. Truman was still president, but Ike had been elected in November. We were back in Peterborough, New Hampshire. The family had grown from four children to eight, with one still to come! A highlight was getting the tree on Christmas Eve. "Judy," a chestnut mare with the shoulders of a workhorse, was hitched to a sledge on which the younger children rode, while the older ones walked, ran, or skied alongside. We would head into the woods in search of the perfect fir or spruce. Arguments would ensue, as each wanted

Papa dancing with "Mitzi" on Christmas Eve

his or her tree chosen. Finally, autocratically but efficiently, my father, with sensible advice from my mother, made a selection. Tears forgotten, we would load the fallen tree onto the sledge and head home. There we would unhitch "Judy" and bring the tree into the house. Decorating was always fun, but the real excitement came when my father brought a bucket of water, which he placed near the tree, then lit candles attached to the branches. We had supper, and got ready for bed. Afterwards, we came downstairs to hang up our stockings and listen to our mother read *A Visit from St. Nicholas*, laughing when she read the words ". . . a little round belly that shook when he laughed, like a bowlful of jelly." By this time, we were so excited we could hardly talk. Then the door to the kitchen opened and in walked Papa leading "Mitzi," the Shetland pony on whom we had all learned to ride. He led her into the living room where a horseshoe was hung next to our stockings. Then Papa raised her front legs and danced about the room, providing a delightful Christmas memory.

Christmas 1962—I was stationed at Fort Dix in New Jersey. Even though Christmas that year fell on a Tuesday, I was able to take a bus to New York to spend the evening and the day with Caroline, whom I had met a year earlier and with whom I had fallen in love. Her parents lived at 86th Street and Park Avenue. Being young and healthy and having just finished eight weeks of basic training, I thought the walk from Grand Central would be easy, not realizing there are twenty blocks to the mile, and I had forty-four to go, wearing uncomfortable black army dress shoes. The temperature was in the twenties, with light snow. I walked up through the slush, in time to get her parents a skimpy little Christmas tree on Lexington Avenue for three dollars.

Christmas 1972—By now Caroline and I were married, and our family was complete. Edward, the youngest, had been born in June of 1971. Sadly, our fathers had died within a year of each other—mine in 1968 and Caroline's in 1969. We were living in the backcountry of Greenwich on Mooreland Road. Sometime around five-thirty on Christmas morning, Caroline and I awoke to a crash in the library, where the stockings had been hung. Sydney, our oldest at six, with his four-year-old sister Linie, had snuck downstairs to see if Santa had come. Linie had been sleeping with one-year-old Edward. Sydney woke her. They put pillows in her bed to make it look as though she were still asleep, then crept downstairs. In their excitement, they pulled down the line of stockings. By the time, Caroline and I got to the room there was paper everywhere and two breathless children explaining to us that Santa had indeed come. I called my mother around seven that morning to tell her all the presents were open.

Christmas 1982—The children were growing up. We were still living in Greenwich, but now on Lake Avenue. By this time, none of the children believed in Santa Claus, but no one wanted to admit he did not exist, for fear it might jinx Christmas day. Son Sydney was home from his first year at Deerfield. Linie was in the ninth grade at Greenwich Academy and Edward was now in the sixth grade at Brunswick. We attended Christmas Eve midnight service at St. Barnabas, about a mile up the road. Christmas was more sedate than ten years earlier. After the presents were opened, we visited Caroline's mother at the King Street nursing home.

Christmas 1992—Our mothers had died two years earlier, like our fathers, within a year of each other. With two children in Europe—son Sydney working in Berlin and Edward finishing a semester abroad at the London School of Economics—we celebrated Christmas at the Lygon Arms, in the village of Broadway in England's Cotswolds. Linie, who had graduated from college in 1990 and was working in New York, flew over with us. The inn dates back to the sixteenth century and is about halfway between the Welsh border and London. During England's Civil War (1642–1651) it had been used as a meeting place by both Oliver Cromwell and Charles I . . . on separate occasions, of course. On Christmas Eve, we walked to midnight services at St. Michael & All Angels. Christmas Day was a feast—breakfast, elevenses, lunch, tea, dinner, and supper. We wondered, how could there be so many thin English people with so many meals served? On Boxing Day there was a hunt, which gathered in the courtyard of the inn. While we all had a good time, our children preferred being home on Christmas morning, a sentiment with which Caroline and I agreed.

Christmas 2002—Another ten years gone by. Caroline and I, now in our sixties, were living in Old Lyme. The children were married, and five grandchildren had appeared. Sydney and Beatriz were living in London with Alex and newborn Anna; Linie and husband Bill Featherston in Rye, New York, with children Caroline and Jack; while Edward and Melissa were in New York City with one-year-old Emma. With the exception of the London crowd, we all had Christmas in Old Lyme. (Caroline and I headed to London a few days later for a belated Christmas with our British grandchildren.) In Old Lyme, we attended the six o'clock service at St. Ann's, where Linie and Bill had been married five and a half years earlier. Stockings were hung, Santa appeared, and Caroline, at age two-and-a-half, had a grand time discovering what delights he had brought. The two other grandchildren were more interested in being fed.

Christmas 2012—Now in our seventies and with ten grandchildren—the last had been born four years earlier. The grandchildren were of an age when they preferred to wake up Christmas morning in their own beds. Because of the sciatica I had developed three weeks earlier in Florida, Caroline and I spent Christmas Eve by ourselves in Old Lyme. On Christmas morning the families of our three children—all sixteen of them, including in-laws—drove up, from Greenwich, Rye, and Darien.

They spent the day and Christmas night with us. Photographs show that Santa once again had appeared, and they show that the grandchildren—ranging from four-year-old Edith to twelve-year-old Caroline—had fun opening presents, playing, and just being with one another. That Christmas would prove to be the last we spent on Smith Neck Road in Old Lyme. From then on, we were with our children and grandchildren at one of their homes, in Rye, Darien, or Lyme.

⁓

Now, nearing eighty and looking back over eight Christmases, one in each of the past eight decades, it is amazing and frightening to see how fast the years flew by. When this saga began, 75 years ago when I was three, Franklin Roosevelt was in the White House, and the population of the United States was 140 million. In 2012, Barack Obama was president and the country held 330 million people. Think of the changes in life's conveniences, medicines, communication, and transportation. The time during which I grew up is as foreign to my grandchildren, as my grandparents' world was to me.

I thank God for the good fortune that has been mine—for the family I have, for the wife that I found fifty-eight years ago, the three children we raised and their spouses, and the ten grandchildren they have produced. It is a fun to look back on carefree days as a child, to remember parents and grandparents, aunts and uncles, and to imagine their childhoods. Coming from a large family, both in siblings and cousins, I remember our playing together—cowboys and Indians, the riding of horses, skiing with my brothers, sisters, and our father—he, at first, on skis brought home from Italy after the war and for which he paid seventy cents. I think of school and college, my teachers and classmates, and of our lives in Greenwich and Old Lyme—of the children growing up. Our lives are full of memories, and each reminds us of how many people and experiences help mold the person we become. I remember the awkwardness of dancing class, ski racing, and the moment I fell in love with Caroline, and I cherish the births of our children, and I treasure the magic they brought to Christmas, which reappeared with grandchildren, and I enjoy the vicarious pleasures they continue to give. I think of that magic that does not change—of eyes round with excitement, dating back generations, as children peek around corners to see what Santa has brought.

Each year, as the calendar closes in on December, we watch favorite old movies: *Miracle on 34th Street*, *It's a Wonderful Life*, *The Bishop's Wife*, and, especially here in Connecticut, the 1945 film *Christmas in Connecticut*, with Barbara Stanwyck, Dennis Morgan, and Sydney Greenstreet. We reread special stories: *The Gift of the Magi*, *The Little Match Girl*, *A Christmas Carol*, and, of course, on Christmas Eve, as we sit with children and grandchildren around the fire with stockings hung from the mantle with care, someone will read Clement C. Moore's *A Visit from St. Nicholas*.

Life takes us on a voyage without a map. Each morning when we rise, we have no idea what the day will bring, where destiny will lead. That boy of three riding around his grandparent's dining room table could not have imagined the places he would go or the offspring for whom he bears partial responsibility. He could never conceive of dreams fulfilled or of disappointments experienced. Perhaps most surprising would be to discover that he now lives less than twenty miles from where he was on his first remembered Christmas. The magic of Christmas is that it knows no age and it knows no place. It is wherever people gather (and have gathered) on the twenty-fifth of December. It is tradition—church services, family, plum puddings, Christmas trees, wreaths, and stockings. It is love. It is, as Churchill said, a time for reflection. And we should never forget that it is Jesus' birth, and His promise of life everlasting. As long as we believe, Christmas will never lose its magic.

Together Alone
April 4, 2020

Together alone
Above and beneath
We are as close
As anyone can be
Now you are gone
Far away from me
As is once
Will always be
Together alone.

"Together Alone," 1993
by Crowded House, New Zealand-Australian recording artists

The coronavirus has driven us to self-isolate, to wear masks, to socially distance, all contrary to man's instincts as a social animal. There have always been hermits, recluses, loners, but most of us thrive in the company of others. The idea is that if we stay apart, the virus will be unable to leap from the infected to the non-infected—a sound bit of advice. Our first day of having to remain on the property where we live was Sunday, March 22; later than others, but still two weeks ago.

Apart from having two newspapers delivered—I used to go out and get four papers—there has been little change in my morning routine. I rise around six or six-thirty, brush my teeth, shave, and exercise. I then wash up, get dressed, and prepare breakfast, which has become my biggest meal of the day. Having read (or mostly read) the papers, I log onto my computer, go over e-mails, scan the news, including what aggregators have sent, print stories I want to read, jot down notes on subjects of interest, edit an essay in progress, and/or start writing a new one.

One change has been a delight. Essex Meadows is located on one hundred acres, with a thousand-acre preserve adjacent. I had been accustomed to walking alone, along trails through the woods and across fields and streams. It was a good place to think. The important—and most difficult for me—aspect of writing is to be clear in what one wants to say. "Clarity, clarity, clarity," wrote E. B. White in *The Elements of Style*, "When you become hopelessly mired in a sentence, it is best to start fresh"—like a walk in the woods! The daily walks still occur but are now accompanied by my wife. Like teenagers, we hold hands, but now to help hold one another up, though the sensuous feeling of intertwined fingers reminds us of long-ago days. We sometimes meet other residents, but most of the time we are alone, together alone. It is a nice feeling, as though we were walking through our own woods, watching our birds, looking at our turtles. We stop to sit, soaking up the sun's rays, getting our Vitamin D, still enjoying one another's company after fifty-six years.

Back in our apartment, we return to our computers—me reading, re-searching, or writing, Caroline reading e-mails, Googling this and that, and checking for sales. Later, after lunch, we'll retire to our den, turn on the electric fireplace, read, write, or watch the news or a movie . . . sometimes fall asleep. What we don't do is go for a drive. We loved to wander the backroads, cross the Connecticut River on the East Haddam ferry, pass by the house in Durham where we lived fifty years ago, shop, and, best of all, visit grandchildren in Lyme, Darien, and Rye, New York. Evenings are short, a light dinner with a movie, thanks to Netflix, Ama-zon, and Apple TV.

A bridge over the Mud River, Essex, Connecticut

It is not that we cannot drive off the property, but it is discouraged. There are about 240 residents at Essex Meadows, most in their eighties, but they range from mid-seventies to over one hundred. Most are healthy, but age carries with it fewer immunities against a disease as contagious as coronavirus, so common sense says stay home, don't go to stores where the virus might lie in wait, maintain social distancing, wear a mask when with others, and practice good hygiene. The staff that works here is special, but because they travel home every evening they must wear masks, so they look like the bandits we pretended to be as children.

Staying home is not all terrible. More time is spent with my wife. I read, dividing my time between fiction and nonfiction. The stay-at-home mandate has made us better understand what is important in life, and it makes one realize that what for us is an inconvenience is a way of life for those in less free countries. There are other benefits. My American Express bill is smaller, and I haven't bought gas for three weeks. We have learned how to use Zoom. Recently, we visited all three families simultaneously, together alone. I had a FaceTime call a few days ago with a doctor, something I never thought I would do. I think of how fortunate we are to live today, with modern medicine and all our technological conveniences, rather than as my parents and grandparents did. We conserve what we have, to make everything last longer and try to avoid waste. All positives. And, say what you will about China, but twenty rolls of toilet paper bought on Amazon last week were shipped to us yesterday from Shanghai!

But negatives come out on top. There is the loss of personal freedom, the missed lunches and dinners with friends, a canceled trip to London and Scotland, and the dishwasher runs more often. Vacuuming and cleaning bathrooms are chores I would rather not do. In this big world of ours, I sometimes wonder: Is anything else happening out there besides the battle against coronavirus? They say that no news is good news, but I am not so sure. As well, there is the uncertainty that comes from a virus we do not understand and against which there is no protection, other than the common-sense remedies that we and others employ. But the biggest negative of being anchored to our homes is the inability to visit our children and grandchildren. Zoom is fine, but you cannot hug a grandchild in a video.

Nonetheless, we are more fortunate than most. My wife and I have each other. Many of our friends are alone. Our furthest grandchildren are eighty miles away, at least when not in college. Friends have children scattered across the country and in Europe and Asia. We are able to stock our larder and entertain ourselves. If feeling lethargic, with Netflix and Apple TV, we can be entertained. Our oldest son brings things we need. We live in a place of caring people and educated, interesting neighbors. "Keep Calm and Carry On" was a poster created by the British government in preparation for World War II. "And this, too, shall pass away" were ancient words Abraham Lincoln used during the Civil War. So, that is what we do: stay calm and carry on, together alone, with the knowledge that this contagion, too, shall pass. Each day gone is one less to wait, together alone.

A Seventy-Fifth Anniversary
May 7, 2020

Can it be true this really is V–E Day?
My mother, in a letter to my father dated May 7, 1945

While V–E Day is celebrated on May 8, the Act of Military Surrender was signed in Reims by General Alfred Jodl, on behalf of Nazi Germany and accepted by General Dwight D. Eisenhower, Supreme Commander of Allied Forces, at 2:41 a.m. on May 7, 1945. When guns finally ceased, Europe had been at war for five years and eight months. Americans had been fighting for three years and five months. An estimated 75 million people lost their lives during those years, including 405,000 Americans.

I was four years old, living at my maternal grandparents' home in Madison, Connecticut, with my mother, two sisters, and a brother. My father, with the 10th Mountain Division, was in Rovereto, just west and north of Italy's Lake Garda. In his *History of the 87th Mountain Infantry*, Captain George Earle wrote: "After the memory of the seared browns of the Apennines and the recent dust of battle, the May colors of the foothills of the Alps seemed unbelievably fresh and vivid." The war in Italy had ended five days earlier.

While some equate our experience with COVID-19 today as our generation's trial, it is not the same. Certainly, healthcare workers, who daily face the possibility of infection, knowingly confront peril. But those of us who "shelter at home" have little in common with foot soldiers in foxholes, airmen in combat, submariners being depth-charged, or marines storming beaches. We wear masks and socially distance.

On May 7, 1945, the war in Europe was over, but the Japanese were still dug in on Okinawa. The next day, President Harry Truman spoke: "This is a solemn but glorious hour." British Prime minister Winston Churchill also spoke: "We must now devote all our strength and resources to the completion of our task both at home and abroad. . . ." An invasion of Japan was planned for the fall, and the 10th Mountain Division was to participate. On May 21, in words that captured his somber mood, my father wrote my mother: "I don't believe there's any use thinking about

Several front pages

getting home for a long, long time." Fortunately, his fears were never realized. The bomb ended the war, and he arrived home on V–J Day.

   None of us chooses a time to be born. It was the fate of the generation
born in the first two-and-a-half decades of the twentieth century that
they were fated to serve in the Second World War. All lives face obsta-
cles, some worse than others, most of which are beyond one's control. We
must play the cards we are dealt. J. R. R. Tolkien, remembering his time
in the trenches during World War I, has young Frodo Baggins, in *The
Fellowship of the Ring*, say to the wizard Gandalf: "I wish it need not have
happened in my time." Gandalf replies: "So do I. So do all who live to
see such times. But that is not for them to decide. All we have to decide is
what to do with the time that is given us." The World War II generation,
in their time, faced incredible challenges, yet they did their duty. They
went without complaint to a fate they knew not.

   On this day, when we remember the victory that brought seventy-
five years of peace to Europe, we should never forget the men and women
who fought to preserve civilization.

Robert Frost and "The Road Not Taken"
May 16, 2020

Two roads diverged in a yellow wood . . .

Robert Frost (1874–1963)
"The Road Not Taken," 1915

The Preserve is a thousand-acre tract that abuts the one hundred acres owned by Essex Meadows. A fire road wends through it. A few weeks ago, Caroline and I came to a fork—two roads diverging, not in a yellow wood as this was spring but at least in a wood. Being New England bred and born, Robert Frost's poem burst into my consciousness.

"The Road Not Taken" is Frost's most famous poem and is considered his most misunderstood. It was written in June 1915 for his friend, the Welsh poet Edward Thomas, with whom Frost would go on long walks when visiting in Britain. "Thomas," wrote the American poet Katherine Robinson five years ago, ". . . was chronically indecisive about which road they ought to take and . . . [he] often lamented they should have taken the other." It was a habit about which Frost teased his friend. When "The Road Not Taken" was published in 1916, Europe was engulfed in a war that would kill 700,000 British soldiers, something a reader should keep in mind. One of the victims was his friend Edward Thomas, who went to France in late 1916 and was killed on the first day of the Second Battle of Arras in April 1917. He was thirty-nine.

The following is the opening stanza of one of Thomas's "war" poems, "Lights Out:"

I have come to the borders of sleep,
The unfathomable deep
Forest where all must lose
Their way, however straight,
Or winding, soon or late;
They cannot choose.

One can see why Frost admired his friend.

Mixed and obfuscated interpretations of "The Road Not Taken," added to its fame. David Orr, poetry columnist for *The New York Times* and professor at Cornell, wrote that Frost "wanted to juxtapose two visions,"

Opposite page: "Two roads diverged. . . ."

the first in which the poet rues that he ". . . could not travel both," and then later congratulates himself, as he ". . . took the one less traveled by." Professor Orr described the poem as a "kind of thaumatrope," an optical toy with two opposing pictures, which when spun merge into a single picture.

Some of the images add to the ambiguities Frost employed. He describes one road "as grassy and wanted wear," yet a few words later ". . . that the passing there/Had worn them really about the same." Then, does the "sigh" in the last stanza invoke disappointment or contentedness? And, in the last line, do the words "And that has made all the difference," refer to a positive or negative experience?

I read poetry without analyzing it—letting imagination and feelings determine what is meant, recognizing my interpretation may change from one day to the next. This poem is short, consisting of four stanzas of five lines, with four stressed syllables per line; the rhyming pattern—ABAAB—is pleasing to the ear. To me it invokes the woods through which my wife and I now walk and reminds me of my youth in New Hampshire, and the mile-and-a-half trek through the woods to my grandparents' summer home. We would pass by a watering hole, proceed through an iron gate, and make our way to the top of the hill, where cows grazed, and white clouds skidded across the blue sky. And on the way, of course, there were birch trees: "One could do worse than be a swinger of birches." One could do worse than be a reader of Frost.

The Home Stretch
June 14, 2020

This is not about going back. This is about life being ahead of you and you run at it!
Because you never know how far you can run unless you run.

Attributed to Penny Chenery (1922–2017)
in the film *Secretariat*, 2010

Using a horse race as a metaphor for life, with its starting gate and finish line, might appear morbid, but that is not the intent. As Benjamin Franklin noted in 1789, there are no certainties other than death and taxes. We are born, we live, and we die. The relevant question is: How much ground do we cover and what do we accomplish in the time allotted? More pertinent, as we come down the home stretch (and something a racehorse never considers), can we look back on our race as fairly run, and did we make time to hug those we loved?

To get around the track—to make it onto the home stretch—is not assured when the race begins. And we cannot forget that there are those who are loaded into the gate and then denied the opportunity to run when the starting gate opens. The length of the course varies, depending on luck, behavior, and genes. Some of us founder, others get bumped, a few break down or become exhausted and retire early. But most of us make it onto the home stretch.

We enter the first turn in our early teens and exit it as independent young adults. The back stretch begins as we leave college, continues on with careers, marriage, and our own offspring, who themselves begin their race. During this period, as we gallop along, our children grow and enter their first turn. Our families and jobs, and schools and colleges for our children, consume our time as the furlongs pass. When our children begin their backstretch, we enter our final turn, during which we witness the marriages of our children and the appearance of our first grandchildren.

As we exit the final turn and head for home, we pass through what is sometimes mislabeled the "golden years." The pace slows but time speeds up. A week, which when we were children felt like a month, has become a year that feels like a week. With the advent of children and grandchildren, our future has enlarged. Lives have been created for which we bear responsibility, and we want to know that they will turn out to be happy ones. But we also recognize, as the song has it, that "the future is not ours to see."

We should not despair, though. The home stretch is filled with family and friends, some new and some old. We have memories to comfort us, a few regrets but mostly good times remembered. We know we have slowed, but our speed has increased. We pray the pounding hooves will slow. The seconds, minutes, and hours tick by in their regular inevitable and foreboding way. We cross the finish line, each in our own time and each at our own pace, not with applause and best without tears, but, we hope, with love and appreciation for a race well run.

The Drones Club
March 7, 2021

Even at the Drones Club, where the average of intellect is not high, it was often said of Archibald that, had his brain been constructed of silk, he would have been hard put to find sufficient material to make a canary a pair of cami-knickers.

P. G. Wodehouse (1881–1975)
"The Reverent Wooing of Archibald"
Mr. Mulliner Speaking, 1929

One thing old people do is rummage through old letters, albums, and photos, dreaming of a past, where memories are often an improvement on reality. The other day, I came across an album devoted to the Drones Club of New York and P. G. Wodehouse. It includes letters, news clippings, cards, etc. The oldest item is a December 27, 1981, article from *The New York Times* on Wodehouse, "A Hundred Years and a Hundred Books," by Charles McGrath. The most recent a June 22, 2017, e-mail from Jane Duncan telling me of the death of Charles Gould in Kennebunkport, Maine, a great friend, world-renowned Wodehousian, and fellow Drone.

Wodehouse's imagined Drones Club was set in London's Mayfair district, in an eternally Edwardian England, where spring and summer were the only seasons, and where neither wars, nor plagues, nor financial crises ever intervened. Plum, as he was called, named the club for the male honeybee whose sole function is to mate with a queen bee. They lounge about all day, feeding off nectar delivered by female workers, waiting for their bit of sex, after which they die— "and therefore is winged Cupid painted blind," as Helena says in *A Midsummer Night's Dream.* Wodehouse's Drones never age. They were as vacuous and as full of fun in the 1960s as they had been in the 1920s when they first appeared. Members included Bertie Wooster, Archibald Mulliner, Barmy Fotheringay-Phipps, Freddie Widgeon, Pongo Twistleton, Bingo Little, Oofy Prosser, and others.

In the Drones Club of New York, we feigned at being members of Wodehouse's Club, but, in truth, we were working stiffs, full of fun, with no hint of aristocratic bearings. Every three or four weeks, for two hours—or maybe even three or four if the bar remained open and baskets

The Dones Club of New York, circa 1985

of rolls for throwing were refilled—we would mimic our favorite characters, quote favorite lines and laugh uproariously. Unlike the Mayfair Club, we integrated, as women's fondness for Wodehouse equals that of men. In fact, my affection for the "Master" came from my mother and my maternal grandmother.

The Drones of New York started with two members, one of whom I knew as director of equity research at a New York insurance company. I was invited to join, along with a friend who was a Wodehouse aficionado. While we never pretended to be as exclusive as Max Beerbohm's Duke of Dorset's Oxford club, the Junta, that "holy of holies," we did not want to be more than a dozen or so. I have a photograph of nine of us taken at New York's Coffee House Club in the mid-1980s, eight men dressed in black tie, with our Queen bee elegantly outfitted in a black gown. Four of those in the photo are no longer with us, including Jerry Gold, our OM (oldest member, not in age, but in seniority). The title OM died with Jerry.

Our first dinners were in a private room at the University Club, where on one memorable occasion a roll bounced off the forehead of a waiter, as he entered the room carrying a loaded tray. A favorite moment was the heated exchange between an elderly member of the Club and two Dronish guests. The subject was hats. The two guests felt proper etiquette allowed for hats to be worn in the lobby of the Club. The elderly member disagreed. (*Gentleman's Gazette* sides with the Drones, stating that a lobby is a public place.) At some point we migrated to the Coffee House Club, a hangout for writers, poets, and playwrights on West 44th Street. It was a cozy place, with the spirits of departed writers mingling with those dining and sluicing. The Drones once put on a skit written by another departed Drone, Ned Crabb, to a bemused, if not amused, audience. Ned, besides being Letters editor at *The Wall Street Journal*, was the author of two novels, *Ralph* and *Lightning Strikes*. Again, we changed venues, this time to the Yale Club, where old Elis, when they saw us coming, asked their waiters for a table change.

The initiation of new members was good fun. We would send the poor sap into the next room, leaving the door ajar so he or she could overhear our discussion. We would make unintelligible but notably negative comments about the person—florid ties, magenta socks, flashy waistcoats. Some of us would complain the prospective member was too friendly, others, not friendly enough. Then, after fifteen or so minutes of contemptuous commentary and personal insults, we would welcome the victim back into the room as a new member. In the case of two younger members, it took a couple of decades to reach full membership . . . in fact, they may still be waiting!

Both Drones Clubs are about the joy of companionship, of common interests. Ours is about being with people who share love and respect for the "Master," P. G. Wodehouse. In this sensitive age, I acknowledge he is a dead, white male. But the truth is we don't care about his color or sex. We care about him because he made (and makes) us laugh, and because he could write dialogue like few others. However, like drones who have mated, time takes its toll. As I leaf through the album, images appear of fellow Drones. Besides the three mentioned above, we have lost two others. One is Jimmy Heineman, who has since joined Wodehouse, Charles, Jerry, Ned, and other Drones, in their heavenly funhouse. Jimmy Heineman had the world's largest private collection of Wodehouse—6,300 items according to a June 14, 1998, article in *The New York Times*. On the centenary of Wodehouse's birth—October 15, 1981—the Morgan Library exhibited treasures from the Heineman collection. Jimmy had begun collecting Wodehouse in 1927 at age ten, when living in Brussels. When the Germans marched in, he and his family left. Four years later, as a soldier in the American army, he made his way back to his parents' home. He found the house intact, the furniture and rugs in good shape, but his collection of Wodehouse gone, so he had to start over. The other Drone we have lost is Owen Quattlebaum, who died too early of cancer in 2002. He had moved to Santa Fe a few years earlier for health reasons. I always loved the fact that on the famed British bookstore Heywood Hill's mailing list his name appeared just above that of the Queen Mother (a Wodehouse fan). She also died in 2002, at age 101. On St. Peter's list, I presume Quattlebaum still precedes Queen.

The death of our OM, Jerry Gold, in 2016 put a damper on our group. COVID-19 halted a planned dinner in New York in the spring of 2020. That plus the difficulty of getting older bodies into New York had meant fewer meetings of Drones. But now, with vaccinations coming, it is time for another dinner, even if we have to come in cami-knickers. God knows, we all could do with a good laugh.

We all belong to groups, from country clubs to eleemosynary institutions. Most have purposes—from providing a venue for golf to helping the disadvantaged. The Drones of New York served no purpose, other than contributing to the joy of its members. But that was (and is) enough. Laughter, it is said, is good for one's health. It tosses one's innards around. We should look for humor wherever we can. I was fortunate to find the Drones forty years ago. It brought friends and served up cherished memories—memories that cannot improve on reality.

1970 and the Connecticut US Senatorial Campaign
March 27, 2021

The 1970 election was a major turning point in Connecticut's political history: not only because of the candidates who were elected that year, but also because it marked the decline of the power of the nominating convention, and the rise of the statewide primary.

The New York Times
March 31, 2006

"If a man is not liberal in his twenties, it means he is heartless; if he is not conservative when he reaches forty, it means he has no head." That sentiment has been attributed to many, including John Adams, the French historian Francois Guizot, Winston Churchill, and my maternal grandfather. Assuming the statement is true (which I will not swear to), I exited my twenties like the final display of a Fourth of July fireworks.

I write of the 1970 US Senatorial campaign in Connecticut. It was the recent obituary of Joseph Daniel Duffey that prompted these remembrances. Born in Hamilton, West Virginia on July 1, 1932, Joe Duffey came to Connecticut for graduate studies at Yale and a PhD in Theology from Hartford Seminary, where he stayed to teach and to become the founder and director of its Center for Urban Studies. As well, in 1970 he was national chairman of ADA (Americans for Democratic Action). He died on February 21 of this year at a retirement community outside Washington, DC.

In that 1970 US Senatorial campaign, Duffey ran as the antiwar candidate, attracting noisy and energetic youth, one of whom was me. He also attracted such well-known people as Chester Bowles, Paul Newman, Larry Kudlow, John Podesta, Joe Lieberman, and a Yale Law School student, Bill Clinton. Duffey was in the forefront of the Civil Rights movement, having organized Freedom Rides in the mid-1960s. He had led an antiwar delegation at the 1968 Democratic National Convention on behalf of Eugene McCarthy. Two years later, the antiwar movement was still going strong, even as the number of US troops in Vietnam, since peaking in 1968, had been reduced by over 200,000 to 340,000, and while deaths—still at 6,173—had declined by 37 percent, from a peak, also in 1968. Nevertheless, civil rights and Vietnam remained issues.

In the summer of 1970, at age twenty-nine, I lived a *Saturday Evening Post*-cover-like life—married, the father of two, working for Merrill Lynch in New Haven, while living in an historic house in the small town (population 4,489) of Durham, Connecticut. I had been honorably discharged from the US Army Reserve two years earlier. While I had grown up in a Republican household, I was exploring political alternatives. A year before, I had registered as a Democrat. In November of 1969, I was elected to the library board, receiving the fewest votes possible—my only experience with elective office. Amidst this milieu, the siren-like call of Joe Duffey's message was intoxicating. A few friends and neighbors like Cheryl Mallinson, A. Reed Hayes, Helena and Keith Hutchison, and I joined the campaign. We joined the Durham Democratic Town Committee. In early June, I was selected to be an alternate delegate to the state convention, which was held on June 27 in Hartford's Bushnell Memorial Hall.

I, of course, had never been to a convention. Though seated in the balcony, I was mesmerized. The activity on the floor, the shouts and smoke were visible, audible, and malodorous. It was democracy in action. When the marching, noise, and haze abated, Alphonsus Donahue, a Stamford, Connecticut, businessman, won the nomination. However, Joe Duffey and State Senator Edward Marcus received enough votes to force a primary, the first in Connecticut's history. Thomas Dodd, a Democrat and the incumbent US Senator, had been censured by the Senate and opted to run as an Independent. Our small group in Durham had helped raise Duffey's profile. We had canvassed our neighbors and printed flyers. We had met with him and his campaign manager Anne Wexler in our home. On one occasion, William Manchester, historian and writer-in-residence at Wesleyan, joined us. None of us had expected Duffey to get the Party's nomination; we were hoping for a primary, and that we got.

Then the work began. Between June 27 and the August 19 primary we were in overdrive. We traveled with Mr. Duffey (his opponents insisted on calling him Reverend) from Durham to myriad venues in other towns. At a fundraiser at the Griswold Inn in Essex, we met Paul Newman, marveling at how short he was and how blue his eyes. On another occasion, also in Essex, we attended a fundraiser at the home of Chester

Bowles, a former Connecticut governor who had been Truman's ambassador to India and Kennedy's under-secretary of state. About a dozen of us were seated in Mr. Bowles' living room. We were asked who would be willing to put up $500. There was no response. Finally, I said I would put up $250 if someone else would match me. Henry Pierce, then president of the Union Trust Company of New Haven agreed. (Incidentally, Henry Pierce was the father of Margot who had been my girlfriend during the summer of 1944, when we were both three.)

That summer of 1970 also included the Powder Ridge Rock Festival. It was held on the Powder Ridge ski slope in Middlefield (population 4,132 in 1970), a rural town adjacent to Durham. This was Connecticut's answer to Woodstock and lasted from July 31 to August 2. Student unrest was persistent. Body bags from Vietnam were returning every day, and the shootings at Kent State had occurred fewer than three months earlier. However, the town fathers of Middlefield canceled the event. Most musicians did not show, but between 30,000 and 50,000 young people did. Accurate descriptions of all that happened were unclear at the time and have been lost in the fog of time and weed. However, from the vantage of fifty years, an article in *Connecticut Magazine* noted: "Certain things are indisputable facts. Drugs were plentiful. Clothes were scarce." My wife Caroline, sensibly, had gone to Rumson with our two young children, leaving me with friends to witness the scene. We spent a couple of hours one evening wandering the fields, and I can attest to the accuracy of the magazine's report.

But the Democratic primary was our focus. Besides raising money, we knocked on doors, sent out flyers, and wrote letters to editors, all in support of Joe Duffey. Al Donahue, who was backed by the Democrat machine, was a wealthy businessman from Fairfield County—the "zipper king," as I recall. A naturally gregarious and confident man, he dressed nattily, in sharp suits and French cuffs—a contrast to many of the residents of the farming community of Durham. Joe Duffey was a man of middling height, slightly balding at age thirty-eight, and of a serious, quiet demeanor, dressed in rumpled suits and sober ties. The primary was held on August 19. When the votes were tallied, Duffey won 43.55 percent of the votes; Donahue, 36.81 percent; and State Senator Edward Marcus, 19.64 percent. We were ready for Weicker, or thought we were.

Once Joe Duffey won the primary, he became the Democratic Party's nominee. But, given his progressive opinions, he was viewed skeptically by many in the Party's hierarchy. About a week after the primary, I attended a six-person meeting in Middletown with John Bailey, a sixty-five-year-old, tough-talking Harvard Law School graduate who had been chairman of the Democratic National Committee during Kennedy's campaign in 1960, the landslide victory by Lyndon Johnson in 1964, and the hapless Democratic convention in Chicago in 1968. This was my first (and only) meeting with a political "boss." Bailey, a Roman Catholic, looked at Joe Duffey, the young Methodist minister his party had chosen, and assured him that if he ran hard and kept to the Party's script, he would not have to worry about a future job. Back-office promises and smoke-filled rooms were eye-opening to this politically naïve twenty-nine-year-old.

Thinking back, I suspect too much of our energy had been used up in the primary. We rested too heavily on garlands we had won. The November election was a three-way race. Senator Thomas Dodd, who had come to fame during the post-World War II Nuremburg trials, ran as an Independent. He was the conservative. Republican Lowell Weicker was a thirty-nine-year-old first-term US Representative and former First Selectman of Greenwich. He was the moderate. Joe Duffey was an untethered progressive. As Duffey supporters, our concern was Weicker, though, in retrospect, we should have paid more attention to traditional Democrats, as Edward Marcus and other Party leaders threw their support to Dodd. There were two debates. An article in *The New York Times* after the second debate, was headlined: "Weicker Assails Two Rivals in Connecticut Senate-Race Debate." In contrast, Duffey was a gentleman. The *Times* reporter wrote about Duffey: ". . . he avoided sharp counterattacks." The job for me and my cohorts was to heckle Mr. Weicker, which we did. When election results were reported on the eve of November 3, Lowell Weicker won with 41.74 percent of the vote. Duffey was second with 33.79 percent. And Thomas Dodd was third with 24.46 percent. Now, decades later, Mr. Weicker lives in Old Lyme with his wife Claudia. When I related my long-ago attempts to disrupt his speeches, he smiled.

The end of a campaign, like any intense effort, leaves one deflated, in need of something to fill the void. After the election, I happened to read Gary Wills's book, *Nixon Agonistes: The Crisis of the Self-Made Man*, which had been published a few months earlier. The book, one must remember, was written two years after Nixon's election as president, ten years after his defeat by John F. Kennedy, and eighteen years after being selected by Dwight Eisenhower to serve as vice president. The book is less a biography and more of a reflection on the struggle that so many have with competing values and aspirations to determine what is right for themselves and their country. In 1963, Robert Frost starred in a documentary, *A Lover's Quarrel with the World*. *Nixon Agonistes* can be seen as Universal Man's quarrel with his country and himself—a struggle to find clarity amid personal and national conflict. While events in the 1972 Presidential campaign relegated Nixon to the ashcan for political crooks, this book, in 1970, caused me to rethink my priorities, including those of a political nature—to use my head as well as my heart.

Joe Duffey was a decent and honorable man, and, despite my political views having changed, I look back on those heady days in the summer of 1970 with pleasure. I am proud to have played a small role, even if not successful. I learned a great deal and met some wonderful people. There are times in our lives that stand out. That summer was one. While saddened by his death, thank you for letting me relive his campaign.

Photos, Children's Books, and the Passing of Childhood
April 24, 2021

Some day you will be old enough to start reading fairy tales again.

C. S. Lewis (1898–1963)
The Lion, The Witch and the Wardrobe, 1950

A framed photo sits on my desk. Taken two years ago at the Seabright Beach Club in New Jersey, it shows our ten grandchildren, cousin alongside cousin. They range in age from ten to eighteen. Recently, looking for a missing picture, I opened the back and out fell half a dozen photos of earlier Christmas cards. The earliest was for Christmas 2003 when there were five grandchildren. The most recent, 2013, with all ten. Looking at the photos I choked up, filled with a sense of loss for the passing of their childhood.

As a grandfather, I am having my third go at childhood. But now, as my youngest grandchild approaches her thirteenth birthday, that most wonderful of all human experiences is about to fade away. My wife and I were fortunate that our three children produced ten grandchildren within eight years, which meant that their childhoods—from the birth of the first on July 10, 2000, to the youngest turning thirteen, which she will do on June 24 of this year—lasted twenty-one years, or 25 percent of my life, too short a time for the joy they bring. Being a grandparent means you get the pleasure without the responsibility. Grandparents bring treats, read stories, and take them on Thomas the Train. Parents must make them brush their teeth, put them to bed, and tell them to turn off their iPhones. Now, looking at the photo taken in 2003 with my daughter and two daughters-in-law holding their babies, and knowing that today all five are in college, I ask, where has the time gone?

One's own children provide a second shot at childhood. Our first arrived in 1966, and the last (the third) turned thirteen in 1984. Those eighteen years represented 40 percent of my then life. While my wife and I were the "heavies," in that we were the ones to discipline our children, we were rewarded with the joys that can only accrue to a parent, in seeing awe in young eyes upon first seeing Santa.

It is our own childhood to which we return as we grow older. During

Children's books from our shelves

those dozen years before the teens arrive, time, like desert sands, stretched toward infinity. It was the only life we knew. Grownups are, of course, necessary. They provide food and shelter, offer shoulders to cry on, and have arms to hug with. But they don't, as we constantly told them, understand us. My mother would admonish me: "Grow up!" How was I to know what she meant? I was a child and spoke and acted as a child. Now, from a vantage point of eighty years, I look back, aided by childhood books and faded black-and-white photographs of people and animals long dead, and I mourn the loss of the innocence of childhood. But I am thankful for memories. I have dozens of pictures with my older sister, younger brother, and sometimes my baby sister, Betsy. Many were taken during the war, most with our mother—on the beach in Madison, Connecticut, or playing with goats in Peterborough, New Hampshire. Time has erased hurt feelings, the scare from once being locked in a bathhouse, recurring nightmares, and the pain of getting my finger caught in a car door. It is the happy times I remember. Riding horseback with my mother, skiing with my father, and doing both with my siblings.

We lived four miles from the village and a mile from the nearest neighbor, so we entertained ourselves. Our house was filled with books, some of which I still own: *Miltiades Peterkin Paul* by Charles Remington Talbot, writing as John Brownjohn, and *An Island Story* by Henrietta Elizabeth Marshall. In the introduction she wrote that the book is "not a history lesson but a storybook." *Daddy Jake* by Joel Chandler Harris (1889) and *Two Little Confederates* by Thomas Nelson Page (1889) belonged to my Tennessee-born maternal grandmother. *Proud Pumpkin* was written and illustrated by Nora Unwin in 1953. She moved to Peterborough from England in 1946, to be close to her friend and collaborator Elizabeth Yates, author of *Amos Fortune, Free Man* and several other children's books. When we moved, these books came along. They include *The Allies Fairy Book*, published after World War I and illustrated by Arthur Rackham. Clement C. Moore's *A Visit from St. Nicholas*, also illustrated by Rackham as *The Night Before Christmas*, was read by my mother and has been read by us to our three children and ten grandchildren.

Over the years I purchased others that I knew as a child: *Mother Goose*, illustrated by Arthur Rackham; *Ginger and Pickles* by Beatrix Potter; *Barnaby* by Crockett Johnson, who appeared in comic strips; *Crock of Gold* by James Stephens and illustrated by Thomas McKenzie. I have original editions of *Uncle Remus* by Joel Chandler Harris; E. B. White's *Charlotte's Web* and *Stuart Little*; *Huckleberry Finn* by Mark Twain; and the four Pooh books by A. A. Milne. My copies of *Alice in Wonderland* and *Through the Looking Glass* were published in 1946 and include the John Tenniel illustrations. I can still recite the poem "Jabberwocky": "'Twas brillig, and the slithy toves / Did gyre and gimble in the wabe. . . ." Who does not get nostalgic for their childhood when rereading the opening sentence in Winnie-The-Pooh: "Here is Edward Bear, coming down stairs now, bump, bump, bump, on the back of his head, behind Christopher Robin." And who does not weep when Charlotte dies: "It is not often that someone comes along who is a true friend and a good writer. Charlotte was both." I could go on. There are over three dozen such books on my shelves. I pull one out, glance through it, and the images that appear are of my own childhood, when there was no past, and the future was indistinguishable from the present.

One's childhood lasts about a dozen years—not long in the average person's lifetime. But memories emerge as we age. And we realize how quickly those years passed by. Childhood cannot be restored but it can be reclaimed through quiet moments spent alone, sifting through old photographs, and turning the pages of a favorite, childhood story. C. S. Lewis, as quoted in the rubric that heads this essay, was right. I am now old enough to read his magical Narnia tales, which I did three years ago.

Eleven Weeks in Europe—1965
May 29, 2021

Short honeymoons are better than no honeymoons, but long honeymoons are best of all.

John L. Davey (1916–1984)
English missionary
Partners in God's Love, published posthumously, April 2007

When Caroline and I married on April 11, 1964, I had ten months of college to go. We were married in New York on a Saturday. On Sunday, we stopped to visit Old Sturbridge Village and then my grandmother in Wellesley before heading to New Hampshire. On Monday I was back in class and Caroline was looking for a job. Once my degree requirements were completed in February of 1965, and a job with Eastman Kodak lined up for June, we took our long-planned, but delayed, real honeymoon to Europe. We had saved $2,000. With it, we bought roundtrip tickets to Paris for $440.80 each and arranged to rent a car for the eleven weeks we would be there. We brought Arthur Frommer's *Europe on $5 a Day*, which had been first published eight years earlier. With a bit over $1,000 in American Express Travelers Cheques, we felt confident in our plans. And we were right to feel so. After buying some gifts for ourselves, including crystal in Venice and a mantle clock in Switzerland, and "a *little* gift for everyone," as Caroline reported to her parents, we returned home with $100.00.

On the evening of March 5, we flew to Paris, with a change in Brussels, seen off from New York's recently renamed John F. Kennedy Airport by my brother and his wife. Once in Europe, our route, in a white, rented Volkswagen, took us south through Tours, Bordeaux, and the beautiful port village of Saint-Jean-de-Luz. We stopped in Madrid for four days and then headed to Alicante, where we spent five days in a pension across a highway from the beach. From there we drove along the Mediterranean coast, arriving in Rome on April 1. We then headed north toward Florence, Venice, and arrived in Vienna in time to celebrate our first wedding anniversary, which we did at Vienna's oldest restaurant, Griechenbeisl. After a side trip to Budapest, we headed west to Salzburg, Munich, Innsbruck, and Zurich. From there we went to Vevey, where my grandfather had been born on February 4, 1873. After visits to Zermatt, Geneva, and Grenoble, we headed south to the French village of Serres, and then back to Paris. After eleven weeks, we flew home on May 21, and were met by Caroline's parents.

There are only two times in one's life when an extensive trip can be taken by most—when first starting out (with a job in hand but a delayed starting date) and when retired. Because of youth, energy, and without the need for the luxuries one expects with age, the former is the most fun. We kept our living expenses low. Toward the end of the trip, I wrote my parents: "We were not staying at any first-class hotels, but they are clean and comfortable, and much more interesting." Rereading letters written to our parents during our belated honeymoon, along with Caroline's diary, photographs, postcards, and the Shell Touring Map we used, has allowed us to relive the trip. The photograph that accompanies this essay

Caroline and me with Pat Bourdery, Serres, France, May 1965

shows the two of us with Pat Bourdery, the sister of a friend of my parents, when we stayed a few days with her in mid-May. She had married a Frenchman in the 1930s. Widowed, she lived on a small farm outside the village of Serres, in the Hautes-Alpes region of southeastern France. Caroline and I would hitch her burro "Kiki" to a small cart and go off on private, romantic picnics.

ح

Our room in Paris, when we arrived on March 6, was small and inexpensive, with the bathroom at the end of the hall and down a flight of stairs. After two or three days, we headed south. At a small pension in Tours, the proprietor informed us that a bath would cost an extra two francs (approximately $0.40). When we told him it was too expensive, he removed the stopper. Not to be denied, Caroline stuffed a T-shirt in the drain. At the Prado Museum in Madrid, we enjoyed the copy of Rubens' *Rape of Europa*, which shows the Phoenician princess Europa being carried off by Zeus in the form of a bull—appropriate, we felt, for Spain. After four days in Madrid, we drove south to Alicante. Caroline wrote to my parents of the landscape: ". . . rows and rows of olive trees. . . . The leaves look as though they were brushed with silver." We booked into the Hotel Costa Azur, at a cost of $7.87 a day for the two of us, which included a private bath and three meals a day. We spent five days, recovering from work and college classes. We enjoyed the beach and swam in the Mediterranean. Our drive east took us through Barcelona, to the walled city of Carcassonne, which had been used by the Germans as a headquarters. We took the tour conducted in French, because, as I wrote my parents, "the tour in English was about 7X as expensive." The next day, in Perpignan, we had our car serviced at the Hotchkiss (my mother's maiden name) Garage, across from our hotel. We continued along the Mediterranean Coast, past Marseilles, with a side trip through Aix-en-Provence, back down to Cannes, Nice, and Monaco, where we saw Princess Grace of Monaco (Grace Kelly) exiting a building. On the road between Aix-en-Provence and Montagne Sainte-Victoire, unable to find an affordable hotel, we slept in sleeping bags under the stars.

Crossing the border into Italy, we drove past Genoa and saw the Leaning Tower of Pisa by moonlight, and then spent the night in our Volkswagen bug. Five nights in Rome followed, where we spent hours in the Sistine Chapel, the Colosseum, museums, and other touristy places. I wrote my parents (both sculptors) that my favorite piece was Michelangelo's *Moses* in the Church of San Pietro. Caroline sent a postcard to my parents from Florence about Rome: "We were there 5 nights and still feel as though we only touched the surface." From Florence, our route took us over the Apennines, and across the Po River at Ferrara, near where my father had crossed twenty years earlier with the 10th Mountain Division. After crossing under German shelling on April 23, 1945, he wrote my mother a week later: "We made the bridgehead across the Po River, which was without doubt the most exciting boat ride I ever took, and I hope I never take another like it." With no one firing at us but hunkered down in our "beetle" just in case, we crossed the Po in under a minute. We spent a few days in Venice, where, on the island of Murano, "we bought," as Caroline wrote to her parents, "some very beautiful wine, liquor and water glasses." We had them shipped to her parents in New York.

We left Venice early Saturday morning, April 10, as we wanted to celebrate our first wedding anniversary the next day in Vienna, which we did. That morning we attended a small church where the Vienna Choir Boys performed. We spent the week visiting St. Stephen's Cathedral, watching the Lipizzaners of the Spanish Riding School at Hofburg Palace, riding the Wiener Riesenrad, Vienna's 212-foot-tall Ferris wheel, driving out to Schönbrunn Palace, the Hapsburgs' 1,441-room summer palace, and Baden bei Wien. On Easter weekend—the next weekend—we joined a tour to Budapest, with fifteen Austrians, two American school teachers, four Italians, and one German. The four Italians and the German were our age, and we became fast friends over the next two days. Still a member of the US Army Reserve, I was nervous (needlessly, as it turned out) as armed Soviet soldiers boarded our bus to check passports and go through our luggage; it was the most obvious contrast between a free Vienna and Communist-controlled Budapest. I wrote my parents: "You should have seen the crowd that gathered and the way they looked when we left. It is all very tragic." Caroline wrote her family: "Boy, count your blessings and be thankful we are who we are and have what we have. You don't realize that until you have crossed over into the Communist section."

Two more days in Vienna and then it was off to beautiful Salzburg, where we walked up to the Fortress Hohensalzburg instead of riding the funicular, to save a few pfennigs. In Munich, we visited with the sister of a friend of ours and had dinner with the wife of a couple we had met in Vienna. (Her husband was in Liberia on business.) Caroline wrote my sister and her husband: "The beer in Germany is delicious, and we seem to be drinking quite a bit." From Munich it was on to Innsbruck, where I skied Patscherkofel, where the 1964 Olympic downhill race had taken place. After getting lost on the way down and having to hike part way back up (too proud and too cheap to take the cable car), I met Caroline at the bottom of the luge track.

We crossed Switzerland, spending a couple of days in Zurich, then moving on to Vevey where we stayed at the Pension Beau Séjour and looked up my grandfather's birth certificate; I am his namesake. We spent two nights at the Hotel Dom in Zermatt, where the view from our room was of the Matterhorn. In a cable car, descending the 500-meter cliff from Sunnegga that looks down on the village of Zermatt, Caroline stood looking out, while acrophobia kept me cowering in the rear. In Grenoble, Caroline felt ill, so I had dinner alone at the railroad station. The next day, she felt better as we drove to Serres to visit the hospitable Madame Bourdery. We had a wonderful, relaxing three days in this mountain village, picnicking and swimming in remote, sylvan pools. From this small village, I sent Caroline a postcard, which she later received at the American Express office in Paris: "Wasn't this the most beautiful part of our trip?" By the nineteenth of May we were in Paris (in a better room than the one we had eleven weeks earlier!), our honeymoon behind us, ready to board Air France Flight 015 on the twenty-first, home to the United States, and back to the real world.

The trip was a once-in-a-lifetime experience. Caroline wrote to her parents from Vienna: "This trip is really wonderful. We are free to leave, and do as we want, and to stay as long as we want." Jobs, children, schools, and many long years of delightful married life, would follow. But we will always have this trip to look back on. A friend, as he got older, once told me: "I regret nothing that I have done. I only regret the things I did not do." Leaving for Europe, as we did, airline tickets in hand, clinging to Frommer's book and the keys to a rented Volkswagen "beetle," we did the crazy thing. But, in doing so, we got to know one another even better, and we made lasting memories from our eleven weeks in Europe.

A Weekend of Music
December 19, 2017

Where words fail, music speaks.

Hans Christian Andersen

A regret is that I cannot sing. My grandfathers could sing, but neither of my parents could carry a tune. And I was never taught to read music. But I enjoy it and envy those who are musical. I marvel at composers who conceive musical notes emanating from multiple instruments, using different melodies, yet harmonizing in a beautiful symphony of sound.

The Hill-Stead Museum—now a National Landmark—is situated on 152 acres in Farmington, Connecticut, just west of Hartford. The house is a 33,000 square-foot colonial revival— "a great new house on a hill top," is the way the American author Henry James described it, shortly after it was built in 1901. The house was built for Alfred Atmore Pope, an Ohio industrialist, and his wife Ada. It was designed by his daughter Theodate, who had attended Miss Porter's school in the same town in the 1880s. Today, the house and its furnishings are just as they were when Theodate Pope (or Mrs. John Riddle as she was then) died in 1946. Inside the house are nineteen rooms, on whose walls hang dozens of Impressionist paintings, including works by Mary Cassatt, Edgar Degas, Édouard Manet, Claude Monet, John Singer Sargent, and James McNeil Whistler.

Caroline and I had been invited by friends, whose daughter is the museum's director, to a Friday night program in early November entitled "From Page to Stage—Selections from Broadway's Early Musicals." It was arranged by Tim Stella who has directed or codirected such Broadway shows as *Phantom of the Opera*, *Jesus Christ Superstar*, *A Funny Thing Happened on the Way to the Forum*, and *Guys and Dolls*. Mr. Stella now lives with his wife in Farmington.

Setting the stage for the evening's performance, mannequins were scattered throughout the house dressed in costumes loaned by the Good-speed Opera House in East Haddam, Connecticut. In the drawing room where we sat was a rare, six-legged Steinway grand piano. On the walls were two Degas, one Manet, and three Monets, including two of his "haystacks." Set in two semicircles were about twenty-five folding chairs for us lucky few. Within those elegant surroundings, one felt like a guest at Downtown Abbey, certain that Maggie Smith would appear, eyeing us the way she does when something isn't right—the wrong shoes, or trousers lacking a crease—but with that hint of an approving smile for what we were about to hear.

Mr. Stella played the Steinway. His wife, Florence Lacey, was one of the company. Ms. Lacey began her Broadway career as Irene Malloy in *Hello Dolly*. Her biggest role was as Eva Peron in *Evita*. Mr. Stella brought with him two other husband-wife teams: John Cudia, a tenor (who played Curly in *Oklahoma* and Cassio in Verdi's *Otello*), and Kathy Voytko (who portrayed Francesca in *The Bridges of Madison County* and Christine in *Phantom of the Opera*), along with Ray Hardman, a baritone (a singer of opera, oratorio, and musical theater), and his wife Kathleen Hardman, who has sung with the Connecticut Lyric Opera, the Juilliard Opera Theater, Marlboro Music Festival, and the Santa Fe Opera.

The program began with John Cudia singing "Oh! What a Beautiful Morning," the opening song in *Oklahoma*. In the movie version, we first hear Curly singing offstage and then watch and listen to him as he comes into view, riding his horse. In this version, there was no horse, but Cudia began the song offstage, and entered the drawing room full-voiced, walking among us.

Fourteen songs were sung, including "People Will Say We're in Love," "Send in the Clowns," "I Dreamed a Dream," and "Bring Him Home." The final song of the evening was, "All I Ask of You," from *Phantom of the Opera*, which depicts Raoul and Christine pledging their love, ignorant they are being overheard. It was sung by the husband-wife team of Cudia and Voytko. In the Broadway musical, it is the song, followed by the menacing reprise sung by the Phantom, that concludes Act One.

The next evening, a (mostly) amateur group called The Six of Clubs presented "King Cole: The Words and Music of Cole Porter." The group was formed in 2010 in New York City by old friends with musical talents, "to perform songs for our friends from 'The Great American Songbook'—the finest American songs of Broadway musical theater and Hollywood musicals." The venue was the First Congregational Church in Old Lyme, with its "perfect acoustics." A reception followed, at the Lyme Academy College of Fine Arts. The current church building was built as a meetinghouse in 1910—the fifth on the same site since 1665—and dedicated by Woodrow Wilson, whose wife was studying at the Old Lyme

Art Colony. The church is home on five weekends a year to one of Old Lyme's treasures, Musical Masterworks, which brings chamber music from the New York Philharmonic to the village of Old Lyme.

Vocalists that evening included Nicholas Firth, baritone, who doubled as narrator; soprano Beatrice (Bebe) Broadwater; Win Rutherfurd, baritone; Rich Miller, tenor; Angela Cason, soprano; and Armenian-American tenor, Brett Noorigian Colby, who has performed in numerous operas in New York and New Jersey. John Hargraves of New York and Old Lyme was on the piano.

Twenty Cole Porter songs were performed, covering twenty-eight years. The earliest was "Let's Misbehave" from the 1928 Broadway musical *Paris*, Porter's first hit, written when he was thirty-six. Three songs were performed from the 1956 film musical *High Society*, apart from *Les Girls*, Porter's last show. "True Love," sung by Bebe and Rich, was his last hit. From the same musical, "Well, Did You Ever," was sung by Nick and Win, with an ad-libbed insertion of Harvey Weinstein at the "Astor Bar."

The program began with the ensemble singing "From this Moment On," from the Broadway show *Out of this World*, which opened in 1950, when Cole Porter was on top of the world. The evening ended with the ensemble singing "It's Delovely," written by Porter for the 1936 Broadway show *Red, Hot and Blue*. In the original cast, Bob Hope and Ethyl Merman sang the song as a duet. Included in the repertoire was "Love for Sale," from the 1930 show *The New Yorkers*. We were told the song had the double distinction of being Cole Porter's favorite and of having been banned from the radio. Cole Porter died in 1964 at age seventy-three. A widower, he had suffered for six years from ulcers that caused his right leg to be amputated. A sad end for a great artist. But his music lives on.

Thinking back on those two evenings—so different yet so alike, one with professional musicians, the other showing what amateurs can do—brought joy, but also a recognition that putting words to my feelings would be impossible— ". . . where words fail, music speaks . . . ," as Hans Christian Andersen wrote. Plato is supposed to have said that music "gives soul to the universe, wings to the wind, flight to the imagination, and charm and gaiety to life and to everything." If he didn't, I will. For I went to bed that Sunday night, unable to hum the tunes, but filled with the gaiety music brings, letting the wings of my imagination take flight into my gaiety-filled dreams.

REFLECTIONS

This section is the longest, with twenty-one essays. It includes thoughts on 9/11, getting older, the fate of print newspapers, doing laundry, and reflections of a recent trip to my hometown. Like most people, I worry about things over which I have no control, but I am, at heart, an optimist, a trait I hope is detectable through prose that I trust is not too purple.

Remembering 9/11—Fifteen Years On
September 11, 2016

Are you guys ready? Let's roll!

Todd Beamer (November 24, 1968–September 11, 2001)
Flight 93 passenger

Sunday marks fifteen years since we were attacked without warning by a small group of Islamic terrorists acting under the authority of al Qaeda. Fifteen years later we are still involved in a war against Islamic extremists. It has been a long time, and there is no end in sight. Thinking about this returns me to my own youth. I was born ten months before Pearl Harbor. Fifteen years later World War II was a distant memory. I was a carefree youth in boarding school. Japan and Germany, our former enemies, were allies and on their way to becoming major economies. General Eisenhower had been president for four years. The economy was booming and, apart from periodically being told to duck under school desks during simulated atomic bomb attacks, life for a fifteen-year-old was peaceful and happy. How long will it be before such idyllic conditions return for today's youth?

The horrific facts of what happened on 9/11 should never be forgotten. More people were killed that day than sailors at Pearl Harbor; more were killed than Americans soldiers on D-Day . . . and those killed on 9/11 were civilians! Speaking before the United Nations General Assembly on November 10, 2001, President George W. Bush said, "Time is passing. Yet, for the United States of America there will be no forgetting September 11. We will remember every rescuer who died in honor. We will remember every family that lives in grief. We will remember the fire and ash, the last phone calls, the funerals of the children."

Take a moment to think back on that day of infamy—the enormity and brazenness of the attacks. Remember those who were lost, those on the planes, those in their offices and the heroes who rushed into the burning buildings. And recognize that the evil that perpetrated those attacks still lives. It must be eradicated if my grandchildren are to live with the hope and optimism that was mine fifteen years after Pearl Harbor.

Retirement Ain't All It's Cracked Up to Be!
October 6, 2016

Retirement is being tired twice, I've thought,
first tired of working, then tired of not.

Richard Armour (1906–1989)
American poet and author

Three weeks from now will mark one year of my retirement. It's an odd sensation—not working—when you've been laboring for over fifty years. One day you have a place to go. The next you don't. Two-thirds of my life was spent on the job.

When young, and prospects of retirement spun through one's mind, they were scenes of palm trees, white beaches, and daiquiris, or vistas of snow-peaked mountains, crystal-clear lakes, and fine wines. In the mind's eye, one saw perfect villages, like Marie Antoinette's Hameau de la Reine. We pictured ourselves hammock-bound in our own Arcadia, with grandchildren seen but not necessarily heard, a book and a beer within reach.

When young we had no idea of the limits age imposes. We could not envision hips not working, or knees without the resilience of youth. Or the mind not functioning with the alacrity of yore. We never thought stairs could get steeper, or that the walk to the mailbox would be longer. Pills, diet restrictions, glasses, incontinence, hearing aids—those were for the "old," something that could not happen to us. We lived ignorant of the march of time. Now, trees we once planted have grown to full height, and the dog is our third, or is it the fourth? What happened to those beautiful, adoring children? They once looked up to me as the fount of all wisdom. Now they look down on my white head with compassion.

We visit our children now and cannot understand why they are not as free as are we. We love seeing our grandchildren, but school, sports, and iPhones occupy so much of their day. Where has time gone? I think of Harry Chapin, and those last lines from "Cat's in the Cradle:"

'When you coming home, son?'
'I don't know when, but we'll get together then, Dad.
We're going to have a good time then.'

Like paper towels, time unrolls slowly at first, then at ever-increasing rates.

When we were young, days were endless—and so were long nights. The roll of paper seemed barely to budge. But as time marched relentlessly forward the paper came off more quickly and the roll became visibly smaller. We now know the past is longer than the future. We find ourselves talking about the "new" generation, their music, noise, and lack of respect for the elderly. It is the circular pathway of life. We forget our own indiscretions—the complaints of our parents now come from our mouths. We yearn for past days when time moved slowly, unaware that it is us, not "youth," that has changed. Like the dray horse that has been put out to pasture, we dream of friskier, coltish days when anything seemed possible—and was.

Yet, in spite of all this, my "retirement" was easy, as for the past few working years I had spent most of my time writing, including essays that had little to do with the work of my firm. It was self-indulgent. Nevertheless, it helped my transition. I spend my time much as I did before, but now working from home, and seeing more of my wife than at any time since we were first married. It has strengthened my love, but my dependency has also increased.

While each generation subscribes to the old Chinese adage that we live in the most interesting of times, what doesn't change are characteristics and emotions that make man man—love, happiness, respect, euphoria, compassion, apathy, grief, and their opposites, hate, anger, jealousy, depression, envy, passion, and joy. It is why the works of Dickens, Austen, Shakespeare, Tolstoy, and the Bible are as relevant today as when they were written. In reading them, we learn more about ourselves—the past, present, and future. The words of Robert Frost's poem shimmer through my mind and bring me back to reality:

> I'd like to get away from earth awhile
> And then come back to it and begin over.
>
> . . . Earth's the right place for love:
> I don't know where it's likely to go better.

The fact is I don't want to live my life over. I consider myself fortunate. I was born at a fortunate time and have been happy with the life I was given.

I am as busy as ever. When not writing, I am reading, traveling, visiting grandchildren, or going for a walk—an opportunity to think about what I am writing. Usually, I bring with me a notepad and pen, stopping every now and then to jot down some word or some thought, knowing that my memory is not what it was. Because I mostly write about current events—politics, the economy, education, climate, global affairs—I like to stay current. And since the media is so biased, I find I must read four or five newspapers every day. But, since I would rather get my news from the papers than TV, I save gobs of time in the evening. I also enjoy reading history—at times thinking education is wasted on the young! —and I recognize the value of reading classics, because of the eternal truths they relate.

So, while retirement may not be all it's cracked up to be, I have found the transition quite pleasant. But no one should expect retirement to live up to its hype. While advice is not part of my purpose ("chacun à son goût," as my mother-in-law used to say), keeping one's self busy is the secret. I should not and will not complain—at least not any more than I already have. I am happy. I don't play cards. I have been lucky in love. Caroline and I are still together after fifty-two years, and we both have our health. The future will bring what it will. I get pleasure from the thought my genes will live on, as we have three children (all happily married) and ten grandchildren. God willing, I will be part of their lives as well.

Getting Older
September 26, 2017

The afternoon knows what the morning never suspected.

Robert Frost (1874–1963)

In 1972, when my daughter was four years old, she noticed a photograph of Caroline and me, as we were leaving the Church of the Heavenly Rest in New York where we had been married eight years earlier. "That's a picture of Mommy and a man," she explained. Caroline looks eternally young, but my hair then was dark, and no glasses perched on my nose. By thirty, my hair had turned white. It was genetic, not marriage related, and I hadn't been scared. I got old early and stayed that way.

I will turn seventy-seven in January. "Growing old," said Billy Graham, "has been the greatest surprise of my life." That has been true for me, given the way age sneaks up. At any rate, I don't feel my age. It is physical and mental, not a chronological thing. By standards of friends at Essex Meadows, the late seventies are young. (Caroline and I are sometimes referred to as "the kids," which makes us feel like yearlings.) On the other hand, our ten grandchildren see us as part of a past they know only through history books and old photos. In fact, we are not singular. We are among about twenty million Americans who have reached our age.

The Population Reference Bureau is a nonprofit organization founded in 1929, specializing in collecting and disseminating statistics for research and academic purposes. In a report dated January 2016, they noted that the number of "senior citizens" (those over sixty-five) will double over the next forty years, and, as a percent of the population, they will rise from 15 percent to 24 percent. Older people are working longer and living longer. I stopped working at seventy-four, though writing essays has me at my computer several hours a day. The average life expectancy in the United States has risen from sixty-eight in 1950 to seventy-nine today. Part of that stems from improvements in geriatric medicine, but the elimination (or reduction) of childhood diseases like polio and smallpox has played an important role. Also, the gender gap has narrowed. Oddsmakers still favor women, but the gap has narrowed from seven years to five over the past quarter century.

But the news is not all good. Obesity rates for the elderly have increased. Poverty remains a problem, though not as acute as it once was. More older adults are divorced, and Alzheimer's, which has already increased in frequency, is expected to triple in the next thirty years. Our economy will be pressured, as Social Security and Medicare rise from the current 8 percent of GDP to 10.5 percent in 2027, according to the Center on Budget and Policy Priorities.

Age does not arrive unattended. It is accompanied by fears—most of which are perfectly natural. We face unknowns. What infirmities will we suffer? How will we die? What happens when we do? In our pseudosophisticated twenty-first-century lives, many of us have given up going to church regularly. So, we are more likely to miss the comfort religion provides, as we consider a world without our presence.

But the magnetism of the future still lures. We may sleep more, but we are not dead. For those of us with children and grandchildren, we know we will live on in their genes and memories. We can argue as to whether their lives will be better or worse than ours. Certainly, they will miss some things we had, but they will enjoy other things we will never know. While politicians and others speak of inequalities and injustices in our culture, there is far less inequality today in terms of living standards, race, creed, and gender than in the 1940s and 1950s. Despite Cassandras who write and speak of the earth's imminent demise due to human-caused climate change, life on Earth is improving, thanks to the spread of democracy and capitalism. The United States Agency for International Development reported last year that global extreme poverty has been cut in half over the past thirty years. While there is obviously much still to be done, the trend is right. But it is a mistake to assume progress will persist unassisted, for nations in the past have miscalculated, as happened in 1914 Europe. Vigilance is wanted. Nothing should be taken for granted.

Growing older involves accepting what we cannot change. It's in the order of things to die. The last leaf does fall from the tree. The Serenity Prayer takes on added meaning: "God, grant us the serenity to accept those things we cannot change, the courage to change the things we can, and the wisdom to know the difference." Age is a time for reflection, to look back at our lives—not to worry about what we might have done, but to recall what we did: To think of those we love. To pass on stories and memories to our children and grandchildren, stories that have lessons or morals: mistakes we made they can avoid; pleasures we experienced they might enjoy; places we visited they should see; and people we knew they should learn about. "It is not true that people stop pursuing dreams because they grow old," wrote Gabriel García Márquez, "they grow old because they stop pursuing dreams."

Change is a given. Our memories are not what they were. Senility lingers offstage. We can recall the smallest detail from our youth, but have trouble with what we did, said, or read yesterday. We empathize with the "Oldest Member," when P. G. Wodehouse has him proffer advice in "The Clicking of Cuthbert": "One of the poets, whose name I cannot recall, has a passage, which I am unable at the moment to remember, in one of his works, which for the time being has slipped my mind, which hits off admirably this age-old situation." Our bodies adjust. Bones become brittle. We make strange bodily sounds. Tendons stretch. Muscles weaken. Bruises take longer to heal. Our chests roll downhill. Where we were once told to stand tall, we are now warned not to fall. Ladders are a "no-no," and stairs viewed warily. The membranes in our spinal column wither and shrink, and so we lose height. As T. S. Eliot wrote:

> *I grow old . . . I grow old . . .*
> *I shall wear the bottoms of my trousers rolled.*

༄

We remember our youth and contraposition it with growing old. In his poem "Youth and Age," E. B. White wrote of the mysteries of youth, contrasted with the crosscurrents that age encounters. "In the spring," wrote Alfred Lord Tennyson in his poem "Locksley Hall," "a young man's fancy turns to thoughts of love." In the autumn, an old(er) man's fancy turns to thoughts of mortality. It is not depression, but rather that past remembrances compete with future aspirations. Having an interest in history and having worked in an industry where numbers are important, I find it fascinating to subtract my age from my birth year. I don't feel old, but January 1865 seems a long time ago. The Civil War was in its last stages, and Lincoln still served as president. By the end of the year, the war would be over, Lincoln would be dead, and slavery would be abolished. Such exercises make me realize, not how old I am, but how young our country is and how connected we are to its past.

My grandchildren love to ask what it was like in olden times. I like to tell them that George Washington was revered but was stiff and formal in person; that Abe Lincoln had a humorous sparkle in his eye, despite bearing the weight of the Civil War; and that Theodore Roosevelt was the busiest man I ever did know, always bustling about, speaking softly, but carrying a big stick. But seriously, their questions are good ones, and I try to respond honestly—to give them a sense of a time gone by, which is now part of the foundation on which their lives are built. None of us is immune from the past, and none of us is indifferent as to the future. It is important we pass on the knowledge that time has allowed us to gain. But, after several questions my eyelids grow heavy. I feel like Lewis Carroll's "Old Father William:"

> *'I have answered three questions, and that is enough,'*
> *Said his father; 'don't give yourself airs!*
> *Do you think I can listen all day to such stuff?*
> *Be off, or I'll kick you downstairs!'*

Aging is part of the process of living. "Life's but a walking shadow," says Shakespeare's Macbeth, "a poor player that struts and frets his hour upon the stage, and then is heard no more." Getting old does not bother me. It is inevitable and preferable to the alternative. I am thankful for the life I have had, for the place and the time in which I was born and the health that has been mine. I was fortunate to be raised in a solid, close-knit family, whose history reflects that of our country. I was too young for Korea and was in the army before Vietnam. After a life on Wall Street, the writing of essays has brought new meaning to my life. The discipline of writing, along with keeping up with the news, and making time to read novels, histories, and biographies have been stimulating and enlightening. I hope (and believe) these activities have broadened my mind. We should never stop learning. Temperance and wisdom are natural trappings of age—not because we are smarter, but because we have time to deliberate. What we lose in spontaneity, we gain in reflection.

I cannot imagine a life without Caroline. We have been married for almost fifty-four years. I cannot imagine life without my children and grandchildren. They mean the world to me. I look at them and see the future. They, their progeny, and generations to come will carry our genes into the future. And I cannot imagine what it would be like not to have friends—some going back decades, others recent.

Going back to that moment forty-five years ago, when my wife and daughter stood before the black-and-white photo in the silver frame, I was amused, not insulted, when my daughter did not recognize the young, dark-haired man with her mother. She needn't be concerned my feelings were hurt. Euripides wrote 2,500 years ago: "To a father growing old, nothing is dearer than a daughter." That is true.

A Visit to the Pinkas Synagogue
and the Old Jewish Cemetery in Prague
March 7, 2019

Six million of our people live on in our hearts. We are their eyes that remember. We are their voice that cries out. The dreadful scenes flow from their dead eyes to our open ones. And those scenes will be remembered exactly as they happened.

Shimon Peres (1923–2016)
Former prime minister and president of Israel

The American Transcendentalist Theodore Parker (1810–1860) was an abolitionist and minister of the Unitarian Church. He is remembered for a quote (since borrowed by others, most notably Martin Luther King and Barack Obama) from a sermon delivered in 1853, when the scourge of slavery still blemished the American Republic: "Look at the facts of the world. You see a continual and progressive triumph of the right. I do not pretend to understand the moral universe; the arc is a long one, my eye reaches but little ways; I cannot calculate the curve and complete the figure by the experience of sight; I can divine it by conscience. And from what I see I am sure it bends toward justice." Grand words—and perhaps true given enough time—but little solace for those who still suffer the evil of man's cruelty to man.

There are places we visit where we witness the sacrifices made by a few for the many: Arlington National Cemetery, the Thiepval Memorial to the Missing of the Somme, the American Cemetery at Normandy, the USS *Arizona* Memorial in Pearl Harbor, and the American Cemetery outside of Florence. There are other, poignant memorials dedicated to the evil that man has inflicted on man: the memorial to the victims of 9/11; Memorial Hall in Nanjing, dedicated to the victims of the Japanese massacre in 1937; the memorial to the Holodomor victims in Ukraine; the Wall of Grief in Moscow that memorializes those killed in Stalin's gulags, the Choeung Ek memorial in Cambodia to victims of the Khmer Rouge; and the Kigali Genocide Memorial in Rwanda. There are other examples of man's inhumanity to man for which no memorials exist, such as the estimated thirty million Chinese who died during Mao Zedong's Great Leap Forward.

In Europe, there are places of remembrance for the more than six million Jews killed during Hitler's reign of terror. More than two dozen concentration camps in Germany, Poland, Ukraine, Latvia, the Netherlands, and Austria are open to visitors. They are reminders of what man is capable of. In Berlin, there is the spacious Memorial to the Murdered Jews of Europe, and in Vienna, a small memorial; but both seem inadequate to the horrors Nazis inflicted. But the one in Prague is different.

The names etched on the walls of Prague's Pinkas Synagogue represent but a small fraction of those who died in the Holocaust. But that adds to its power. One gazes with incomprehension on the names, including birth and death dates of 78,000 Jews from Bohemia and Moravia who were killed by the Nazis. Families are grouped; so that the elderly are mingled with children and grandchildren. Upstairs is a room housing two dozen pictures drawn by children taken to the Terezin ghetto, which became the Theresienstadt concentration camp. There they were held before being shipped to Auschwitz for extermination. A woman named Friedl, who was also imprisoned at Theresienstadt, taught some of

Old Jewish cemetery

the children to draw, suggesting remembrances of their homes and families. Her purpose was to distract the children from a world where no arc was bending toward justice. Below the drawings are the names of the child-artists and the date—when known—of their death. Before she was sent to Auschwitz, Friedl gave the tutor of the Girl's Home two suitcases of the children's drawings, thus they survived. It is impossible to walk through this display without tears.

My seventeen-year-old grandson Alex saw this synagogue as a "sacred place," now devoid of members, "an empty temple dedicated to God," he said. As he looked at the names and of the drawings of children not much younger than himself, he said he "felt regret for the fallen darkness," and that he was "filled with melancholy for the fathomless acts of cruelty." Usually voluble, he was silent as we walked into the cemetery. It is the personalization that makes this hallowed ground so sacred. These are not just names on a wall, but real people who laughed and cried; people who loved and were loved; people who worked, prayed, and played. This is not simply a memorial to those who died a brutal, senseless death. In these rooms, we look death in the eye and see the evil man can do.

The Old Jewish Cemetery in Prague is Europe's second oldest; it was used between 1439 and 1787. The oldest gravestone is that of rabbi and poet Avigdor Kara. About 200,000 Jewish people lie interred within its small enclosure, with graves in some places twelve deep. It is so crowded that tombstone abuts tombstone. In 1784, Emperor Josef II (at that time, Bohemia was part of the Austro-Hungarian Empire) banned burials within the city walls for hygienic reasons, so the cemetery was closed. During World War II, while other Jewish cemeteries in Prague (and elsewhere) were destroyed, with Nazis using tombstones as target practice, this one was saved. Hitler wanted one preserved as a museum, but also as a warning that he had the power (and the willingness) to annihilate whole segments of society he felt undesirable.

Prague is an ancient city and Jews were long part of its culture. Evidence of settlements in the region date back more than 7,000 years. Around 500 BC, a Celtic tribe named the area Bohemia and the river Vltava, both names which are still in use. By the eighth century Slavs had settled in what is now Prague and in the ninth century construction began on a castle on a hilltop across the river. In 926, the foundation was laid for the city's first church, on the grounds of what is now St. Vitus

Cathedral. It was outside that church where Wenceslas (a duke, never a king, and later a saint)—made famous in the Christmas carol "Good King Wenceslas"—was murdered on orders from his brother in 935.

Adding to the sorrow is learning that Jews had lived in this area for a thousand years. The first recording of Jews in Prague dates to the tenth century. While subject to periodic pogroms, by the early eighteenth century they represented, according to Wikipedia, a quarter of the city's population. In fact, according to the same source, there were more Jews in Prague at that time than in any other city in the world. The 1930 census showed 117,551 Jews living in Bohemia and Moravia (essentially today's Czech Republic). Today, about 4,000 Jews live in that same area. A people and their culture are gone.

The Great War was less than twenty years in the past when the Munich Agreement (September 30, 1938) ceded the Sudetenland—a narrow strip of land, wrapping around the north, west, and south of what is now the Czech Republic—to the Nazis. In March 1939, in violation of that agreement, Hitler's Wehrmacht invaded the rest of Czechoslovakia. Britain and France sat silent. Six months later Hitler invaded Poland and World War II was underway.

Tears welled in my eyes, as I walked out of the Old Jewish Cemetery and into the "old town," in all its aged beauty—with its narrow streets, small squares hidden behind stone arches, open plazas, and beautiful buildings. I thought of the more than six hundred years of a culture that had been lost—a way of life that came to a cruel and final end, during six years of German occupation. Looking at the walls of names in the Pinkas Synagogue, I thought of lives and loves that were lost, and of loves and lives that would never be. I could only imagine the size of a building needed to list the other five million, nine hundred and twenty-thousand names not memorialized here. I can only pray that the arc of history will bend toward justice. It must. If we do not believe that, what, then, is there to believe?

Nostalgia
January 1, 2020

It's a funny thing about coming home. Looks the same, smells the same.
You realize what has changed is you.

Eric Roth (1945–)
The Curious Case of Benjamin Button, 2008
(A screenplay adapted from the short story by F. Scott Fitzgerald, 1922)

Nostalgia suggests a sentimentality for the past, typically for a period or a place with happy personal associations. The aphorist Mason Cooley once wrote, perhaps more harshly than he had to: "Nostalgia paints a smile on the stony face of the past." It is true; memories focus on the positive.

Asked by grandson Alex a few months ago to describe what it was like to grow up in the late 1940s and early 1950s, I found myself stymied. How does one sift good memories from bad? What is truth, and what is simply a memory one wants to believe? World events do not define our childhood, nor does the political scene, nor even the state of the economy, though all three affect our lives. It is, rather, the relationships with our parents, siblings, friends; it is school, and what chores and play consumed our days. It is the small things, like the instance when I was twelve and found a rare dollar warming my pocket. By chance, the baker who delivered bread and pastries from the back of his van twice a week drove up the driveway. I foolishly bought a dozen jelly donuts and more foolishly proceeded to devour them without sharing. My reward was a stomachache and a future aversion to jelly donuts.

Thinking of one's childhood creates a tendency to look for a past purified through the filter of time. Which memories are real, and which exist only in our minds? Unhappy memories become tucked away and more difficult to recall than those that are pleasant. In *Educated*, Tara Westover's 2018 coming-of-age story written when she was thirty-two, the author uses half a dozen footnotes to explain that her memory may be faulty. And she was thinking back only twenty years. In Thomas Wolfe's novel *You Can't Go Home Again*, he explored the changing scene of American society, a universal subject not bound by time or place. Just as in George

Webber's case (Wolfe's character in the novel), my hometown is different than it was sixty years ago. Oh, yes, the bank and the post office are still on Grove Street and the library is still on the corner of Concord and Main, just across the Contoocook River. But the innards are different. The Unitarian Church, where I went as a child, is now the Unitarian Universalist Church, but it still sits on Main Street and Summer. The elementary school I went to has been gone for over fifty years, but I remember the dark and scary windowless coat closets, and the strict, unsmiling but capable teachers.

The layout of the streets is the same, but the movie theater is gone, as are the depot where we used to pick up feed for the animals, and Derby's, the department store where one could buy anything from clothes to appliances. The biggest store in town today is the Toadstool, a bookstore started by a younger, enterprising brother almost fifty years ago. The physical changes are more cosmetic than foundational. And, yes, Summer Street still becomes Middle Hancock Road, as one drives north. Whit's tow, where I learned to ski, has been replaced by affordable housing units. The Dodge Place, where my parents went to live after they were married in 1938, is still four miles from the village on Middle Hancock Road, about halfway between Peterborough and Hancock. The house and barns still stand, but seemed sad when we recently drove by, in need of paint and too quiet, absent the activity and noise that nine children provided. Seen only in my imagination were the goats and horses that once grazed and played in the fields behind. The pair of peacocks that adorned the front yard have gone to wherever peacocks go when they die.

Two recent events caused a wave of nostalgia to sweep over me and reminded me that I had never answered Alex's request. The first was a painting in a gallery in Old Lyme. It depicted a summer cabin, such as one might have rented seventy years ago, in the early postwar years, usually on a remote lake or pond. It was a simple structure, in need of repair. One could envision a hand-driven water pump in the kitchen, no electricity, and an outhouse out back. An aunt and uncle had such a place on Martha's Vineyard when I was young, a place I remember with a dozen of us packed into three or four small rooms. It had a bunk room for children and a half-mooned two-holer thirty feet from the back door. It dawned on me that my grandchildren might never know a life where children entertain themselves in small boats, swim in a lagoon, dig for clams, play hide-and-seek, and fly kites. The second event was watching a pickup game of hockey on Exchange Club Pond in Old Saybrook. As I watched the half-dozen skaters pushing a puck around, I thought back to clear, cold winter days when I played similar, informal games of hockey on Fly Pond in Peterborough, not far from where Summer Street becomes Middle Hancock Road. When we got bored with hockey, we would race up to girls and, in a preteen and early-teen mating ritual, yank off their hats and make them catch us. Once my brother, sister, and I watched mournfully as a truck bound for Benson's Wild Animal Farm carried the carcass of one of our horses that had died a couple of days before. Later, as the sun began to set, we would light bonfires and toast marshmallows for s'mores. "It is strange how much you can remember about places like that," E. B. White wrote in his essay "Once More to the Lake," "once you allow your mind to return into the grooves which lead back."

Our childhood lives are long when living through them but pass by quickly in retrospect. In my case, my childhood ended when I was fifteen and went off to boarding school. While I have some memories of when I was three and four, most are between five and fifteen—not a lot of years to form the character we become. But those moments leave an indelible impression. "Sometimes you will never know the value of a moment until it becomes a memory," wrote Dr. Seuss. I can think of hundreds of such moments—stopping at Howard Johnson's in Brattleboro, after a day of skiing at Hogback or Bromley, with coffee for my father and hot chocolate or a slice of apple pie for us; playing in the hayloft; being summoned from Miss Flagg's second grade class by a fifth grader who told me he was going to beat me up after school, and being terrified the rest of the day; swinging on birch trees, à la Robert Frost, as we walked through the woods; spending three days and two nights with my mother in the White Mountains, when I was going through puberty; playing on the swings my father had built in our backyard; posing for our artist parents; picking wild strawberries in the field next to the "Brick House" (now the Well School); climbing on skis the two and a half miles from Pinkham Notch to "Howard Johnson's," a lean-to at the base of Tuckerman's Ravine on Mount Washington, and the next day hiking up Wildcat. I recall a family trip to Stowe when I was twelve, and the embarrassment of having to share a bed with an aunt. I remember cantering "Judy" along dirt roads, with a younger sibling on "Mitzi," a smart, stubborn Shetland who refused to let the much bigger "Judy" pass. And then years later, after I had left home, I remember that my mother cradled "Mitzi's" head in her arms as the pony took her last breath. These memories tear through my conscience like an icy dagger. You can't go home again, as Thomas Wolfe titled his posthumous novel. You can, but only in your memories.

As children, we lived dual lives. Most of our time was spent in Peterborough, but now and again we would go to East River in Connecticut or Wellesley, Massachusetts, to visit our grandparents. It was a glimpse into a world different from the one in which we lived. In Wellesley where my father grew up, our grandparents lived in a large Victorian house, the one in which my grandmother had been born in 1875, and which became hers when she married in 1907. The house is on Lake Waban, which is really a pond. My mother's parents lived in a large house on Long Island Sound in Madison, Connecticut. It had its own beach where we swam and lay on the beach. There was a barn and a paddock for the animals my mother brought with her. Before my grandfather died in 1947, he would take us to "Bruin's Lair," a hidden spot, perfect for a friendly bear, in the woods on a path beyond the barn. There we would leave treats which were always gone the next day.

But most of my growing up was in New Hampshire. It may only be the way we remember things, but life seemed simpler in those days. We lived four miles from a village of 2,500 people. There were fewer timesaving devices; an absence of technology meant board games that required shared participation; we read poetry and memorized short speeches, like Lincoln's Gettysburg Address. At school, we were reminded almost daily of the Ten Commandments, the Lord's Prayer, and the Pledge of Allegiance. While patriotism was common and mingled honor with love for country, it was temporarily hijacked by Senator Joseph McCarthy in 1950, when he used it to falsely accuse dozens of loyal Americans of Communist sympathies, solely to advance his dark vision. Personal freedom was a bicycle. Mine came in the form of an "English" bike on my thirteenth birthday, in January 1954. Taking it out, I skidded on the ice, and went over the handlebars, bruising my jaw. The lesson: Don't ride a bike on the ice! Nevertheless, our parents worried less as to our whereabouts than do parents today. That didn't mean they loved us less, just that they felt the environment more secure, and they trusted us.

Expectations were less, in terms of what government would provide.

It was assumed we would look after ourselves. On the first day of school in Mrs. Fitzgerald's fifth grade class, it was expected I would check on my sister, Betsy, who had just entered Mrs. Morris's first grade class. In our small town there was little diversity in terms of race or religion. Inequality existed. Some kids' parents lived in bigger houses; some kids were smarter and others stronger and more agile. We didn't philosophize; we were realists. We knew that some had the ability to hit a ball further and to run faster. Some received better grades and others were more diligent. We got into wrestling fights and confronted bullies. Misogyny, I am sure, existed, but was absent in our household where we children saw our parents as equal partners. That was also true of our grandparents. Our grandmothers, we all knew, were as accomplished as our grandfathers. Our parents and grandparents were lovers of nature and the environment. They made sure we cleaned up after ourselves when picnicking or camping.

It is important to keep the past in perspective—what we should treasure and what we should leave behind. The British journalist and author of *The Rational Optimist*, Matt Ridley, wrote recently in *The Spectator*: "We are living through the greatest improvement in living conditions in history." Extreme poverty has declined around the world. Despite violence on TV shows, in movies, and in video games, and the religious tyranny that persists in much of the world, there is less violence today than at any time in history. In rich countries, consumption of minerals and fossil fuels has declined, while standards of living have increased. Reliving the past should not cause us to forget how improved our lives are today. The misty past hides blemishes and the future will have its share. We remember the good and suppress the bad, like getting out of bed in the winter in a house with no central heat; bringing in the kindling, so my father could light the wood stove; having to share a bedroom with three siblings. Clothing material was less friendly: snowsuits became soggy and woolen mittens never kept hands warm. In winter, we had to carry water from the house to the barn for the horses and goats. Picking blackberries on Cobb's Hill or highbush blueberries in the "next field" were chores, not outings. Even so, there were moments of fun. I remember once returning from an afternoon of picking blackberries and seeing goats peer out from every downstairs living room window. Someone—it could not have been me—had forgotten to shut the gate to the field and had left the door to the house open.

We forget, also, how improved we are as a country—how civil rights and women's rights acts of fifty years ago have bettered the lives of minorities and women; how Medicare and Medicaid have helped the elderly and the poor. Polio was a constant dread for parents and children before the Salk vaccine was first administered in 1955. In 1950, according to the CDC (Centers for Disease Control and Prevention), childhood deaths were 29.2 per 1,000. By 1999, that had dropped to 7.1 per 1,000. Pneumonia and influenza killed 314 children per 100,000 as late as 1960. Forty years later, the number was 8 per 100,000. While nuclear weapons still exist, we no longer—perhaps naively—live with the threat of annihilation from the Soviet Union. Changes in communication have been revolutionary. Today, when on an errand, without my cell phone I feel naked.

We all have a past. It helped form who we became. It is important for us who are older to communicate our story to succeeding generations for it helps in their search for identity. But we must keep it within reason; the past should not dominate our lives. The last sentence in F. Scott Fitzgerald's *The Great Gatsby* has pertinence: "So, we beat on, boats against the current, borne back ceaselessly into the past." Fitzgerald refers to an innate desire to recapture the past—that we might correct mistakes we once made. But the truth is the past is the past. It is something to cherish, to learn from, and then move on.

In this season, as the old year goes out and the new year comes in, we sing Robert Burns song, "Auld Lang Syne," an evocation of the past: "Should old acquaintance be forgot / And never brought to mind?" The answer is no, we should not forget old acquaintances, but it is unhealthy to dwell too much on the past. So, Alex, it is the present and the future over which we have some control. That should be your focus.

Happy New Year!

Fate of Print Newspapers
August 14, 2013

*Every time a newspaper dies, even a bad one, the country
moves a little closer to authoritarianism.*

Richard Kluger (1936–)
American journalist and Pulitzer Prize winner

Institutions trapped in the past will be truncated by the future. Print
newspapers are among businesses most affected by forces of creative
destruction wrought by the internet and social media. E-mailed news
alerts; texts from friends, colleagues, and social media; all-news all-the-
time radio and cable news networks are available twenty-four hours a day,
on smart phones and iPads. Why purchase a print newspaper?

Why indeed! Circulation is declining. In the United States, week-
day print circulation has shrunk from a high of 60 million in 1994
to 28 million today. Rumors of the possible sale of the *Los Angeles
Times* to the Koch brothers brought consternation on the Left. Last
week, sales of two newspapers were announced. One was the sale of
The Boston Globe, along with its website and affiliated properties, to
John Henry, principal owner of the Boston Red Sox. The price was
$70 million—a substantial reduction from the $1.1 billion paid for the
paper in 1993 by the New York Times Company. Mr. Henry may
be able to transition to a digital format, but if all he does is drive attendance at Fenway Park, his bargain-basement purchase may pay off.
Promoting one's interests through owned media has been going on for
years. In Thursday's *Investor's Business Daily*, Monica Showalter noted
that Napoleon, in the late 1790s, when still an "obscure general fighting Austrian and Prussian troops on the Italian border," bought two
newspapers to promote his troops' successes. In 1804 he had himself
proclaimed Emperor.

The more interesting transaction, however, in terms of what it may
mean to the future of news dissemination, was the sale of *The Washington
Post* to Amazon founder Jeff Bezos. Mr. Bezos used about one percent of
his estimated $25 billion net worth to buy *The Washington Post* from the
Graham family. According to an analysis in last week's *Barron's*, the news-

paper has been losing money for at least four years. It is expected that they will lose about $100 million this year.

What was Jeff Bezos' motivation in purchasing *The Washington Post*? Was it a bet on nostalgia—a rich man's way of embedding in amber a form of communication that has existed for four hundred years, but is at risk of becoming irrelevant? Does Mr. Bezos have political ambitions, so sees the *Post* as a platform for pushing an agenda?

The Washington Post began life in 1877. In 1933 it was bought by Eugene Meyer, who in 1947 formed the Washington Post Company. It went public in 1971 and two years later, Warren Buffett invested in the company. The company obviously benefitted by diversifying, away from dependence on the newspaper, into education and cable and network television. In *The New York Times*, Ross Douthat wrote in his weekly Sunday column that it is possible to date when the opportunity to become a new-media paper of record for political coverage came and went: ". . . it happened in 2006 when John Harris and Jim VandeHei left the Post to found Politico." Today, as Mr. Douthat notes, "Politico rather than the *Post* dominates the D.C. conversation." Mr. Bezos' challenge will be to keep the *Post* relevant.

As to the question, is print dead? Again, any answer is a guess, but I think not. However, it will never be the same. By the time a newspaper is on the stand or in your mailbox, much of the news is stale, having already been covered by all-news-all-the-time radio and TV and, of course, the ubiquitous internet. Print news, in the future, will not be so concerned with breaking news, as with analysis—more in-depth reports on cause and effect—and, of course, opinion. Daily digital readership at *The New York Times*, at 1.1 million, is approaching its print readership of 1.9 million. In terms of US dailies, circulation declined by one percent last year but, thanks to price increases, circulation revenues rose 5 percent.

Creative destruction is a natural phenomenon in economic progress, and newspapers are a current and visible victim. Aside from being cheaper and faster to produce, digital media can direct news with more precision toward a targeted audience—an appeal to advertisers but harmful to thoughtful consumers. Democracy depends on a free and diverse press that offers factual news and thoughtful opinions. There will be no shortage of news and news sources. The risk, as I see it, is that individuals tend to watch and read that which supports preconceived opinions. That could lead to increased partisanship. I hope I am wrong and perhaps I am, but that is my fear.

Man versus Machine
November 11, 2013

The real question is not whether machines think but whether men do. The mystery which surrounds a thinking machine already surrounds a thinking man.

B. F. Skinner (1904–1990)
Contingencies of Reinforcement: A Theoretical Analysis, 1969

Since the Industrial Revolution, man has had to combat the growing intrusion of machines. The trend has accelerated. When chess grandmaster Jan Hein Donner was asked what tactic he would employ, if asked to play against a computer, he replied: "I would bring a hammer."

An increased use of machines has been one factor in the widening spread of incomes. In an article for the London *Times*, Daniel Finkelstein wrote: "In the past 30 years, the proportion of national income taken as a reward in the form of wages has fallen while the proportion due to owners of capital has risen. And this has happened all over the world, pretty much regardless of what politicians have tried to do about it." The owners of technology stand in stark contrast to the individuals who are replaced. But there is nothing new in this. Machine intelligence has been incorporated into increasingly sophisticated programs and algorithms. But "creative destruction" goes back further. In 1776 Adam Smith, in *The Wealth of Nations*, wrote of the division of labor, as it applied to the manufacture of pins. It was the start of specialization in manufacturing, enabled by machinery.

In 1913, with the production of the Model T, Henry Ford created the assembly line. On a slow-moving conveyor belt, workers performed the same task repeatedly, mind-numbing for the individual but the innovation decreased the time to produce a car by a factor of eight. The result: more cars for consumers at lower prices. In 1914, Ford began paying his assembly-line workers $5 a day, double the average wage. Increased production meant increased employment. Higher-paid workers and lower car prices meant increased demand.

Machines are able to do things that in the past required humans. In *The New York Times* investigative reporter Charles Duhigg's new book, *The Power of Habit*, a man walks into a Target outlet, complaining that the store had been sending his daughter discount vouchers for baby clothes and equipment: "She is only in high school," he complained. A few days later, the man was back, apologizing. His daughter was indeed pregnant, a fact known by Target's computers because of her buying habits, but unknown to her father.

Algorithms allow American Express to notify us when our spending habits change. If we cannot be reached to confirm a purchase, our card is canceled. Artificial intelligence allows surgeons to operate remotely and drones to kill terrorists in remote locations with little collateral damage. Google's driverless cars have traveled well over 200,000 miles. A programmer and a PC can replace a company's entire marketing department, using algorithms to measure and massage consumer behavior. Machines replaced the London Stock Exchange twenty-seven years ago, and today handle much of the trading in New York Stock Exchange-listed securities. Engineering and design firms have been affected, improving output per employee, much as manufacturing firms did two and three generations ago. Newspapers face competition from bloggers, as dangerous and illusive to them as terrorists are to western democracies. Massive Open Online Courses (MOOCs) are revolutionizing the college experience—reducing prices and increasing the value of selected professors but eliminating the "college experience."

Wall Street has applauded many of these productivity improvements, as improved earnings generate higher stock prices. But corporate productivity and individual productivity are on different axes. Machines, in saving labor costs, improve a business's bottom line. On the other hand, and especially as machines become increasingly "smart," they carry out tasks that negate the need for skilled labor. The consequence, as Tyler Cowen noted in his new book *Average is Over*, is an America that has divided in two—the children of "Tiger Mothers" and the rest. Mr. Tyler wrote that markets are exceptionally accurate at measuring an individual's economic value, sometimes with "oppressive precision." Thus, we have millions of individuals who have less value to the economy than they had a few years ago. As individuals, we either master technology, or it becomes our executioner.

There are no easy solutions. Income redistribution is one option sometimes offered, but social engineering does not address the cause. The need is to find a balance in a fluid and ever-changing society. The best answer lies in education, and people need to adapt and to anticipate the "next new thing." Government can expand educational opportunities—promoting

My father with our dog, "George,"
and a goat looking out the window of our 1938 Chevrolet

the competitive advantages of vouchers and charter schools, for example, and the need for technical schools and community colleges. Equality of outcomes cannot be mandated without greatly reducing overall wealth, and voiding liberty. But government can encourage opportunities so that motivated children, no matter their financial resources, will not be disadvantaged. Creative destruction, we should not forget, is an unpleasant but natural aspect of human development.

No one should throw up their hands in despair. There are personal characteristics that will always be in demand—aspiration, motivation, creativity, adaptability, fearlessness, and a willingness to take risk and to work hard—none of which are (as of yet) replicable by a computer. Those characteristics drive future success. In a global world, it is increasingly easy to move production facilities and financial assets; location matters less than it did.

The world is the way it is. As the Chinese maxim has it, teaching an individual to fish is better than providing that person a fish. Dependency leads to poverty of desire. A friend recently sent this quote from British novelist, J. B. Priestly: "I have always been delighted at the prospect of a new day, a fresh try, one more start, with a bit of magic waiting somewhere behind the morning." Good words to wake up to. One thing is certain—a hammer is not a realistic option.

Pandemic by the Numbers—My Numbers
June 21, 2020

Worry is like a rocking chair. It gives you something to do but never gets you anywhere.

Erma Bombeck (1927–1996)
American humorist

We have all found different ways to spend the time we have been given but didn't want. My wife and I have now spent thirteen weeks on Essex Meadows' campus. Caroline had bloodwork done on March 19, which was our last time off the property. During these past three months temperatures outside have ranged from below freezing to the high eighties. While my official temperature has remained normal, my internal engine has become heated. I have enjoyed time with my wife, and have kept busy writing, but the monotony of the days is numbing, so I thought it would be fun to jot down some things done, how I've sent my days—a look at the pandemic by numbers—my numbers.

I am amazed at how much was done, and how little must have been done before. It should not be a surprise, because lists tend to exaggerate. If I had kept all the empty wine bottles from last year, my wife would call AA. Nevertheless, a quote from P. G. Wodehouse, when he was interviewed in 1974 by the *Paris Review*, comes to mind: "I know I was writing stories when I was five. I don't remember what I did before that. Just loafed, I suppose." I was not loafing before the pandemic arrived; it is the listing that makes it seem that way. However, every number is an estimate. As to whether the numbers are underestimated or exaggerated, I leave for the reader to decide:

600,000—estimated steps taken in walking about 250 miles (two and a half miles a day = 6000 steps) on Essex Meadows property and on trails through The Preserve. The Health App on my iPhone keeps tally.

30,000—estimated words written during the past three months, which include fifteen Thoughts of the Day, six Essays from Essex, and five Burrowing into Books reviews.

3,250—crunches and about half as many leg lifts, based on five workouts a week.

1,625—pushups (see above).

1,000—number of sheets of paper used (and thrown away) in writing the aforementioned essays.

300—essays by others, printed and read, on matters dealing with politics, culture, education, and climate.

200—newspapers read—two daily newspapers (*The Wall Street Journal* and the New London *Day*, and the Sunday edition of *The New York Times*).

175—an estimate of poached eggs cooked and eaten.

100—TV movies or shows watched after getting into bed, usually around 8:30 pm.

26—number of times we received groceries and sundries from our son and his family who live in Lyme, Connecticut.

25—loads of laundry. (When we moved to Essex Meadows, my wife put me in charge of laundry.)

10—books read and begun—five fiction, five nonfiction.

5—Zoom calls with our children and grandchildren.

3—virtual high school graduations.

3—pedicures given my wife.

3—number of pounds lost since the lockdown began.

2—webinars participated in, courtesy of the Hayek Institute of Vienna, one to be broadcast this Thursday.

1—miles driven around the parking lot, trying to prevent batteries from dying, unsuccessfully in one car.

0—our Master Card bill for April and May. (I cannot say the same for American Express.)

Of course, time for this exhaustive list was made possible because of things not done:

We have not visited our children's homes.

We have not hugged our children or grandchildren in over a hundred days.

We have not filled our cars with gas since mid-March.

We have not been in a grocery store, drugstore, newsstand, liquor store, dry cleaner, barbershop (my hair is getting bushy), dentist, or doctor for three months, though both my wife and I did have one experience each with telemedicine. (We prefer real visits.)

We have not been out for dinner, by ourselves or with friends.

We have not been to the beach club, which opened with "proper distancing" on Memorial Day.

I have not been able to attend weekly ROMEO (retired old men eating out) lunches for three months.

A planned trip to England and Scotland in April was canceled.

At some point this nightmare will end, and we will look back as at a bad dream. But while in its midst, we should make the most of what we can do to keep ourselves productively (or even nonproductively) occupied. Do not lose faith and do not worry. Remember, what some have rent asunder, others will rejoin.

Humor in Politics—Remedy for Tension, Tonic for Victory
March 19, 2014

A person without a sense of humor is like a wagon without springs.
It's jolted by every pebble on the road.

Henry Ward Beecher (1813–1887)
Congregationalist minister and abolitionist

We live in a world addicted to twenty-second sound bites. Nastiness consumes politics. Putting on a white tie for the annual Gridiron Club dinner, and then reading preset jokes that mock others is not the same as unscripted, self-effacing jokes.

Humor, when used preemptively, disarms opponents, and defuses tense situations. When we think of American presidents and humor, the two that come to mind are Abraham Lincoln and Ronald Reagan. However, there are others. James Garfield, who only served as president for two hundred days in 1881 before being shot by an assassin, once said: "Man cannot live by bread alone. He must have peanut butter." Franklin Roosevelt, in the midst of the Depression, curiously advised: "When you get to the end of your rope, tie a knot and hang on." Harry Truman, when asked about his choice of careers, answered in his earthy manner: "My choice in life was either to be a piano player in a whorehouse or a politician. And, to tell the truth there's hardly any difference." President Eisenhower once noted, "A sense of humor is part of the art of leadership, of getting along with people, of getting things done."

Political humor is most effective when it flows naturally. It is not designed to make a point, with the butt of the joke often being the teller. During the 1960 campaign, candidate Jack Kennedy, amid complaints about his wealth, once told reporters: "I just received the following wire from my generous Daddy, 'Dear Jack. Don't buy a single vote more than is necessary. I'll be damned if I am going to pay for a landslide.'" Kennedy had an ability to be warm, self-effacing, and authentic. On another occasion, amid calls of nepotism regarding the appointment of his younger brother to be Attorney General, he replied: "I see nothing wrong with giving Robert some legal experience as Attorney General before he goes out to practice law."

Coolidge, with his famous dour expression—"looking like he had been weaned on a pickle," as Alice Roosevelt Longworth allegedly once described him—is not remembered for his humor. While he could be funny, he was noted for being spare with both language and time. Once asked about dealing with unwanted guests, he explained he would let the visitors do all the talking. No matter what they said, in about three minutes they would hesitate, at which point he would say, "Thank you," and the meeting would end. A story, told by Amity Shlaes in her biography of the thirtieth president, *Coolidge*, shows another side of the man. Mr. and Mrs. Coolidge were taking separate tours of a government farm. Mrs. Coolidge expressed interest in a prize rooster. The farmer told the president's wife that the rooster was able to perform the sex act several times a day. "Tell that to Mr. Coolidge when he comes by," said Mrs. Coolidge. When Coolidge approached the rooster, he asked, "Is it with the same hen every time?" No, said the farmer. It is with a different hen each time. "Be sure to tell that to Mrs. Coolidge," said the president.

Lincoln is generally considered the first American president with a sense of humor; though I am sure historians and presidential scholars have other candidates. Robert Mankoff, writing in *The New Yorker* in November 2012, claimed that what we consider humor today in the 1840s and 1850s was called "the sense of the ridiculous." Being funny and being cruel often "went hand in hand." But there is nothing cruel about humor when it is unassuming. When accused by Stephen Douglas, in one of their famous debates, of being two-faced, Lincoln responded: "Honestly, if I were two-faced, would I be showing you this one?" When some officers complained about the drinking habits of General Grant, Lincoln noted: "Well, I wish some of you would tell me the brand of whiskey Grant drinks. I would like to send a barrel of it to my other generals."

Lincoln used stories as parables to make points and deflect contentious questions. Walt Whitman thought it was "a weapon which he employ'd with great skill." Richard Henry Dana, United States attorney for Massachusetts, complained that the president resorted to parables when principles were needed. "Storytelling was at the core of the president's character," explained Louis Masur, director of American studies at Trinity College, in *The New York Times* two years ago. Melancholy, according to Mark Twain, is the basis for humor. Certainly, that was true in Lincoln's case, as he suffered from depression, made worse with the burden of the Civil War and the death of his young son Willie in February 1862.

In our generation, it was Ronald Reagan who was master of humor to disarm opponents. Being accused of not working hard, Reagan replied: "I have left orders to be awakened at any time in case of a national emergency—even if I'm in a Cabinet meeting." In response to a comment by Walter Mondale in a 1984 debate, Reagan replied, "There you go again!" Mondale's point was forgotten in the laughter that ensued. In the same year, Reagan countered the claim that at seventy-three he was too old. He did so before Mr. Mondale could strike. "I am not going to make age an issue of this campaign," he quipped. "I am not going to exploit, for political purposes, my opponent's youth and inexperience." Mondale, like everyone else, laughed.

Now, in a time of instant replay and endless reruns of all indiscretions, politicians are reluctant to speak extemporaneously. We learn little about the responsiveness or the mental agility of candidates. When a politician goes on shows with Stephen Colbert, Conan O'Brien, or Jimmy Kimmel, jokes are scripted and then read. The purpose is to humanize the robot-like figure we are supposed to endorse. Reading jokes is not the same as having the easy self-confidence that allows some to laugh at themselves, or to tell humorous stories to illustrate a point.

Reagan, as governor, once met with a group of students, claiming his (Reagan's) generation didn't understand them. "You don't 'get it.'" As these young students noted, they grew up in an age with nuclear weapons, jet planes, and space travel. "You're right," replied Reagan, "We didn't have any of those things. We invented them."

Veteran's Day, 2020
November 11, 2020

In Flanders fields the poppies blow
Between the crosses, row on row,
That mark our place; and in the sky
The larks, still bravely singing, fly
Scarce heard amid the guns below.

"In Flanders Fields," May 3, 1915
John McCrae (1872–1918)

While this is a day for remembering and honoring those who serve and have served in our nation's armed forces, it is remarkable how distanced most of us have become from military personnel and from the duties they perform that help keep us free. It was not always so.

Out of a population of 132 million Americans in 1940, sixteen million served in World War II, 12.12 percent of the population. Today, 1.4 million Americans are on active duty, or 0.4 percent of today's population. In 1960, before Vietnam but when the draft was still in force, 2.5 million Americans were in the armed forces, or 1.4 percent of the then population of 181 million.

In 1980, 18 percent of all American were veterans; today the number is closer to 5 percent and declining. Demographics are changing. The number of male veterans is expected to fall by half over the next two decades, while the number of female veterans is expected to double. In 1975, according to a 2017 Pew Research study, 81 percent of United States senators were veterans; today that number is closer to 20 percent. This has consequences, as love of country and respect for our history and flag are more common among veterans than among the population as a whole, according to the same Pew study.

Both of my grandfathers served in the military—my Grandfather Williams during the Spanish-American War and my Grandfather Hotchkiss as an honorary colonel in the First World War. Neither saw combat. However, combined, their six sons and three sons-in-law all served in World War II, and all except one—a medical doctor—in combat. One was wounded—on Okinawa—but all survived. I am the only one of my parent's nine children and their eighteen grandchildren to have served in the military, and I was only in for six months of active duty, prior to Vietnam.

"Freedom is not free" is an over-used idiom, but it bears a truth—over a million Americans have died in our nation's wars since independence from Britain was declared in 1776. Its words are engraved on the Korean War Memorial in Washington, DC. Our nation, the lamp that lights the world, would not be here were it not for those who went to war, some of whom sacrificed their lives, so that freedom would reign.

We should, perhaps, consider reinstituting the draft. We do not face a major war, but preparedness is always crucial, and national service has other benefits. It helps youth mature. It gives youth a sense of their country. It is an equalizer, in that all recruits are treated the same. It makes no difference to your drill sergeant if you are just out of Harvard, a recent graduate of Illinois Central Community College in Peoria, or if you are off the streets of Chicago. He (or she) does not care if you are black, white, Hispanic, or Asian. He does not care what religion you might be, how much money you have, or who your father and mother are. He cares about one thing—preparing you to be ready for what lies ahead.

As we take a few minutes this day, remembering at the eleventh hour of the eleventh day of the eleventh month when the "guns of August" were finally stilled, we should discuss and debate the value of a draft, for ourselves and our youth, and how it might bind us all closer to this nation we call home, the United States of America.

Thanksgiving Thoughts, 2020
November 24, 2020

On Thanksgiving Day, we acknowledge our dependence.
William Jennings Bryan (1860–1925)
Speech to the American Society, London, November 26, 1903

Thursday is Thanksgiving, a uniquely American holiday. (And, with sheltering in place, unique to this year!) Like Christmas and Easter, it is a religious holiday, as the Pilgrims who we celebrate, and who landed in what is now Plymouth, Massachusetts, four hundred years ago this month, were escaping religious persecution. But, while the Pilgrims were Christians, this holiday is spiritual in a broader sense. The God we thank when we sit down to feast may be whatever God we choose. After all, according to a 2019 Pew Research survey a third of Americans—35 percent—do not consider themselves Christian, but all celebrate Thanksgiving. So, no matter one's religion, if any, all give thanks for the good fortune to live in this country.

The Pilgrims were Puritan refugees from England, where they had wanted a simpler and purer church than the Church of England offered. They went to Leiden, Holland, around 1610, but returned to England to sail from Plymouth to the new world in September 1620. Not one of the 102 passengers or thirty crew members would have made that trip without a belief that God would guide them. They crossed three thousand miles of uncharted ocean to an unknown destination, to arrive in November as winter was taking hold.

The Mayflower Society, made up of 150,000 descendants, estimates there are thirty-five million people who could trace their ancestry back to the *Mayflower*. The concept of the power of compound interest proves the point. Of the passengers and crew members, about one third died that first winter. Most of the rest (about eighty people) stayed. Since I can trace my ancestry back to William Bradford, I know that I am, through his son and granddaughter Mercy Steele, the eleventh generation—William Bradford would be my nine-greats grandfather, his genes diluted by the fact that I also carry the genes of another 2,047 nine-greats grandparents! (Apparently through William Bradford, Clint Eastwood and Hugh Heffner are cousins!) Because many children died in infancy, most families were large, as children were assets. If one assumes, for sake of argument, that each family had three children and that twenty-three of the seventy-five survivors had children one gets to thirty-five million in the thirteenth generation, my grandchildren's generation. The actual number of *Mayflower* descendants may be far higher. Other ships, carrying mostly British subjects, began arriving in 1621. Conclusion: The Mayflower Society, to which I do *not* belong, is not exclusive.

As science and technology advanced, we became wealthier, but more secular. Science uncovered mysteries, explaining the color of our hair and eyes, our height, intelligence, and athleticism. But what gives some people drive and determination, and others none? What provides a moral sense? Can those characteristics be learned? Why were we born and not someone else? What guided a specific sperm to a specific egg? Was it by chance? There are mysteries of life still unsolved. Their presence does not mean an absence of science. Is it not possible that there is a power greater than us?

There is a bigger message in Thanksgiving, something that gets lost in the materialistic world in which we live. Civilities, those actions and words that allow societies to coexist and prosper, are disappearing, and as a result, we banish tolerance and respect, and we forget to give thanks for what we have. Growing up in the late 1940s and early 1950s, we were taught simple rules: to honor our mothers and fathers, to respect our elders, and to obey our teachers. We were taught the Ten Commandments and had to memorize the Golden Rule. We were told to be polite, to look the person addressing us in the eye, and to shake hands firmly. We did not have to agree with everyone, but we were expected to dissent with civility.

Technology has made the world smaller. A two-month voyage from Plymouth, England, to Plymouth, Massachusetts, now takes about five hours. Through social media and smartphones, we are more connected than ever, but are personal relationships more intimate or less? Have we substituted knowing a few people well for knowing a lot of people casually? Are there roses that go un-smelt? Are there consequences to this haste? In his college newspaper, *The Brandeis Hoot*, my grandson, Alex Williams, in a column titled (with thanks to Dr. Seuss) "Oh, the Places We'll Go," recently wrote: "In many ways, we don't want to make the world a smaller place, to drain it of its wonder and deprive it of its sense of dimension and sprawl." We need time to think, time to read, time to appreciate one's own culture and time to talk to strangers and learn something of others. What a difference a hundred years has made. When my maternal grandfather was responsible for the U. S. Rubber Company's plantations in the 1920s, his business trips would last nine months. He traveled by steamer to Britain, then through the Suez Canal to what is now Malaysia, the largest producer of rubber in the world at the time. He would return, moving east across the Pacific, through the Panama Canal, down to Brazil and up the Amazon to Manaus, before returning to New York. The downsides of such trips are obvious. My mother spoke of how much she missed him. It is not a life I would have wanted. But he had time to reflect and to learn other cultures. When I knew him in the 1940s, he always took time to take us grandchildren to "Bruin's Lair," a small clearing in the woods where he, who had shot tigers in Bengal, would tell us of the friendly bear we believed existed, but never saw.

Thanksgiving is a day to slow down (except for those cooking), a time to reflect. "For the technologies that are inspired from wonder," as Alex wrote in his essay, "their object should not take us to a place as fast as possible, but to service the more imaginative inclinations of our human experience." Thanksgiving is a day to express gratitude. In his London speech from which the rubric is taken, William Jennings Bryan, a great fan of our independence from Britain, reminded his listeners of our dependence on so much. "We did not," he said, "create the fertile soil that is the basis of our agricultural greatness; the streams that drain and feed our valleys were not channeled by human hands . . .; we did not hide away in the mountains the gold and silver. All these natural resources . . . are the gift of Him before whom we bow in gratitude tonight."

On this particular Thanksgiving, we celebrate without our extended families, but we should still think of the freedom that is ours. We should think of those less fortunate, and of those who live in countries less free. We should remember those who have gone before us, and we should be thankful for our ancestors, from whence and whenever they came. They struggled to come here so their descendants would live in religious and political freedom and have opportunities for success. We should recall and be thankful for the culture and values taught us by our parents, for they comprise the glue that binds our society.

Happy Thanksgiving!

On Turning Eighty
January 31, 2021

At twenty, a man is a peacock; at thirty a lion; at forty a camel; at fifty a serpent; at sixty a dog; at seventy an ape; at eighty, a nothing at all.

Attributed to Baltasar Gracián (1601–1658)
Spanish Jesuit, writer, and philosopher

On this date eighty years ago, my mother delivered a baby boy, with the assistance of Dr. Robert Salinger, at Grace New Haven Hospital. It was 3:00 p.m.; the baby was named for his father.

All babies, it was once said, looked like Winston Churchill. Whether that was complimentary to Churchill or the baby, I never knew. But what was true for many was apparently also true for me. Two days before the commencement of Operation Dragoon on August 15, 1944 (the invasion of southern France), my mother's youngest brother, my Uncle Joe Hotchkiss, was in command of LST 601. Churchill was there to wish the men Godspeed. He stood aboard a barge that came down the column where Uncle Joe's ship was anchored. My uncle wrote to his parents of Churchill: "Smiling and waving, he passed within fifty feet. He was in his blue playsuit looking just as much like little Sydney Williams as he could."

Regarding the rubric quoted above, it hurts that a man who never made it to sixty should refer to one who has turned eighty as a "nothing at all." Of course, when the average person meets 10,000 people in a lifetime it means I may have met approximately 0.00014 percent of the world's population. Those I do know or have known may have something to say about me. The rest could care less whether I am a peacock, a camel, or an ape. So perhaps Gracián was right. To most of the world I don't exist.

Nevertheless, I do, and I feel good. I am healthy and blessed in my family and friends. Yesterday morning I did my regular (five days a week) series of exercises, which includes fifty crunches and twenty-five push-ups. Yet, my grandchildren look at me, knowing I am a relic of yesteryear. I can hear them reworking those lines from Lewis Carroll: "You are old, Pop Pop Williams, my grandchild said, and your hair has become very white. And yet you incessantly stand on your head. Do you think at your age it is right?" Well, my hair has been white for fifty years, and I do not stand on my head. Staying upright is my focus! Nevertheless, I look forward, with chin out, to whatever the future offers. Bring it on, I say!

Of course, there are things given up as one ages. For example, I gave up skiing in my seventies. One advantage of giving up something like skiing is that time and memory exaggerate past reality. I never danced down the deep powder on Vail's Bolshoi Ballroom with the grace I see in my mind. But so what? It's my memory. We all have a little Walter Mitty in us. And age has other advantages. It excuses one from the complexities of high tech. When I had trouble logging onto the portal my accountant wanted me to set up for my "organizer," my complaint brought forth the following e-mail response: "Bonny, please send Sydney a paper organizer."

However, eighty doesn't seem that old when I look back at the speed with which the years have passed. Was it really seventy-seven years ago that I saw my father board a train in New Haven that took him to Texas and thence to Italy with the 10th Mountain Division? Can it be that seventy-five years have passed since I enrolled at Miss Lindeman's school in Peterborough, New Hampshire, or that sixty-five years have gone by since I met John Harper, my roommate at Williston Academy? Has it really been fifty-seven years since the Reverend Dr. J. Burton Thomas, pronounced Caroline and me man and wife at the Church of Our Heavenly Rest in New York? Can our youngest child be turning fifty this year? Our grandchildren were born yesterday, so why are five of them in college? Where has time gone? Photographs remind us of what once was, just as in our memories the people we once knew live on. In his 1958 book, *Things Fall Apart*, the Nigerian author Chinua Achebe wrote: "A man's life from birth to death was a series of transition rites, which brought him nearer and nearer to his ancestors." There is truth in that. At night, before nodding off, my mind wanders back to earlier days.

When I turned thirty, my wife threw a birthday party. There was a sense of youth left behind for the more serious job of being a parent: recklessness, out; responsibility, in. Indicative of the age, a fight broke out in the dining room over something, the importance of which has evaporated. At forty, Caroline threw another party—less rambunctious. Our children were getting older. There is a photo of me in a cowboy hat, with a silly, bourbon-induced, grin, contemplating the onset of middle age. There were no fisticuffs, just a bunch of men and women having fun. There have been three other parties celebrating the passage of the decades, with the time between each, while numerically the same, getting shorter.

When we're living through it, time passes quickly. On the other hand, the eighty years before I was born seem long ago. Consider what those years brought and how far away they seem: the Civil War and the assassination of Lincoln. Custer's Last stand in June 1876. The assassination of two more US presidents: James Garfield in Long Branch, New Jersey, in 1881, and William McKinley in Buffalo, New York, in 1901. Teddy Roosevelt's ride up San Juan Hill, in 1898. Kitty Hawk, North Carolina, in 1903, with the Wright Brothers' first flight. Doughboys sent to France in 1917 to "make the world safe for democracy," not realizing the war would give rise to Mussolini and Hitler. The "Roaring 20s" and the Great Depression. Hitler's invasion of Poland in 1939 and the start of World War II.

In a letter to Edward Dimmitt, in July 1901, Mark Twain wrote: "Life should begin with age and its privileges and accumulations, and end with youth and its capacity to splendidly enjoy such advantages." I have been one to repeat the oft-quoted line that youth is wasted on the young, but I fear Twain is wrong for one fundamental reason—not knowing our fate helps keep us going.

Time is sobering, as it exhibits both the alpha and omega of life. In those eighty years before I was born, all but one of my great-great-grandparents died, as did all but one of my great-grandparents. And my parents and grandparents were born. Since my birth, all have died, along with two sisters and one brother. In Hannah Rothschild's book, *House of Trelawney*, Tony Scott, an aging, bachelor art dealer, reminisces: "One of the worst things about aging is that if you stop, there's a danger you might never get going again; muscles seize up and then every movement is uncomfortable." We cannot let that happen. Walking with my wife in the woods around Essex Meadows is a lifesaving antidote.

In his 2016 book of essays, *Senior Moments*, Willard Spiegelman wrote, darkly in my opinion: "We come into the world alone, with a cry. We exit alone, to confront the eternal silence. The fun, all the pleasure and adventure, lies in between." More succinctly and less poetically, a friend used to make the same point: "It is not the destination in life that is important, but the trip." But who knows? Perhaps the future is more exciting? John Kendrick Bangs suggested the party continues. In his 1896 book, *Houseboat on the River Styx*, he wrote of Charon, whose job was to transport 'shades' across the River Styx, from the land of the living to Hades. He takes command of the houseboat, which is filled with well-known personages, from myriad cultures and multiple centuries, who socialize together. The house committee includes Sir Walter Raleigh, Cassius, Demosthenes, Blackstone, Doctor Johnson, and Confucius. Who wouldn't want to mingle with that group? Bangs was having fun of course, but the dead do live on in the memories of those who knew them. After my Grandfather Hotchkiss died in 1947, my grandmother told me to remember him and to do so often. "For," she said, "when you do, he will come alive, in your memory." She was right. He does.

In "Morituri Salutamus," Henry Wadsworth Longfellow spoke to his fiftieth reunion class at Bowdoin:

> *For age is opportunity no less*
> *Than youth itself, though in another dress.*
> *And as the evening twilight fades away*
> *The sky is filled with stars, invisible by day.*

⌁

And on that note, with a future lit by stars, these reflections on completing eighty years come to a close. But I go on.

Rituals/Habits
February 19, 2021

Rituals keep us from forgetting what must not be forgotten and keep us rooted in a past from which we must not be disconnected.

Tony Campolo (1935–)
American pastor, author, and spiritual advisor to President Clinton

The chains of habits are too weak to be felt and too strong to be broken.

Samuel Johnson (1709–1784)

While a thesaurus considers "ritual" and "habit" to be synonymous, there are differences. Rituals have roots in the past, ties that bind one to history, tradition, family, and community. Habits are learned or are of one's own creation, often adopted subconsciously, like starting each day with a cup of coffee.

The word ritual stems from the Latin *ritus*, a noun meaning a religious observance or ceremony. Webster's defines the word as "an established procedure for a religious or other rite;" but it also includes as a definition: "any practice or pattern of behavior regularly performed in a set manner." Habit stems from the Latin *habito*, meaning to dwell, to live. However, it is defined today as: "An acquired pattern of behavior that has become almost involuntary as a result of frequent repetition." Rituals are performed with deliberate intent: going to church every Sunday or pledging allegiance. Habits, on the other hand, are taught, like being kind to strangers and saying please and thank you. Rituals we accept as part of our culture. We are criticized for bad habits and praised for good ones. Despite Samuel Johnson's admonition, in the rubric above, habits can be controlled (with effort), whereas rituals exist whether we partake or not.

"Habits are automated behaviors that we repeat over and over," wrote Marco Badwal, cognitive neuroscientist at the University of Amsterdam. Good habits must be taught and performed subconsciously, like manners and taking prescription medicines. They provide social mobility, better health, and allow us to focus on the complexities of life. Rituals are the perpetuation of obligations, like daily exercise or Sunday dinner with family—duties we should perform and activities we enjoy. P. G. Wodehouse once wrote: "Poetry is good, but tea is better." He was referencing the English ritual of afternoon tea with scones and clotted cream. But an Englishman's ritual may be no more than a rare and pleasant interlude for a tourist. Rituals, in some cultures, can be horrific, like honor killings, a ritual still practiced in Pakistan, or genital mutilation, a ritual experienced by Ayaan Hirsi Ali when a young girl in Somalia.

Nevertheless, most rituals are good, at least in the United States, for they allow a continuum in a discordant age—from the baptism of a grandchild to the inauguration of a new president, from singing the national anthem at ball games to saluting soldiers on Memorial Day. Warren Buffett sets aside a certain amount of time every day just to read and think, a ritual he claims helps him avoid impulsive decisions. A ritual I have is to read only for pleasure after seven o'clock in the evening. While I have not been a regular communicant for several years, church service is a ritual I miss, as it provides quiet moments to pray for those we knew and loved and, to use a modern maxim, because it offers time to "think outside the box" regarding problems and current events. Whether my absence is laziness, or due to ministers trying to be relevant to "woke" congregations, is not pertinent to this essay. I did, however, find illuminating a line in Joseph Johnston's recent book, *The Decline of Nations*: "Religion is more than the private worship of a deity; it is the strongest support for morality and the spiritual bond of a society." Attendance at religious services lies on the positive side of the ledger when judging rituals.

Habits, on the other hand, get us through the tedious parts of living, allowing us time to be creative and take risks. Most habits are good, but others less so, like biting one's nails, picking one's nose, or changing lanes on the highway without signaling. And we must be wary that they do not become so ubiquitous that they interfere with free choice, something the satirist Ambrose Bierce warned against in his definition of the word in *The Devil's Dictionary*: "Habit, n. A shackle for the free."

But to get back on track and describe the difference between habit and ritual through my own routine: Most mornings, my habit is to rise before six-thirty, listen to the news as I brush my teeth, and shave. A ritual is to exercise five days a week before showering and dressing. A post-pandemic habit has been to take my temperature every morning. A second daily ritual is to drive to the corner drugstore to buy my newspapers before returning home to perform my third ritual—fixing and eating breakfast.

On Thursdays and Sundays, I do laundry, a chore my wife assigned me when I retired. It is certainly not a ritual, but neither is it a habit . . . at least not yet. One habit from childhood returns every winter: In putting on my jacket, I hold the cuff of my sweater in my hand, so it won't bunch up in the sleeve of the jacket—a lesson from my first grade teacher.

Rituals keep us linked to positive (mostly) aspects of our common culture; their link to the past helps us live in the present and prepare for the future. Habits allow us to live civilly and to free our minds to inspiration. Wearing a mask is not ritual (unless one is robbing a bank), but neither, in my case, is it a habit. It is not ritual that I write essays, but it has become a habit. Can rituals become habits? I leave that to superior minds. I have gone on long enough.

Sleepless in Connecticut
February 27, 2021

A ruffled mind makes a restless pillow.

Charlotte Bronte (1816–1855)
The Professor, published posthumously in 1857

Insomnia is not uncommon as we age. Bodies that have been functioning for several decades begin to show natural signs of wear. The brain hormone melatonin, which regulates the circadian rhythm that determines our sleep cycle, may become affected by age. Being neither a doctor nor a scientist, I don't pretend to understand our internal workings. I experience them and marvel at them.

An Irish proverb says: "A good laugh and a long sleep are the best cures in the doctor's book." I like that advice. I laugh a good deal but do not always sleep well. I am not alone. James Hamblin wrote in the December 21, 2020, issue of *The Atlantic*: "Roughly three quarters of people in the United Kingdom have had a change in their sleep during the pandemic, according to the British Sleep Society." (The Brits seem to have societies for every conceivable situation!) I suspect polls in the United States would show similar results. Back in September, the University of California/Davis Health Center issued an article headlined, "COVID-19 is wrecking our sleep with coronasomnia." They cite the fact people, working from home, are up at "weird hours" and that we need "variety in our activities." I am not up at weird hours, unless one counts those trips to the bathroom to satisfy Nature's call, but the pandemic *has* limited the variety in my life. They (the UC Davis people) offer a lot of useful tips: keep a daily routine, avoid your smartphone before going to bed, get exercise, cut back on news and social media "especially in the evening," go easy on alcohol, and don't nap.

I get the exercise I need, at least I think I do. I no longer listen to the evening news. (I read the morning papers.) I stay away from social media, which I don't find especially social. Perhaps I do shut my eyes, or as a friend once said, "check my eyelids for holes," for a few minutes in the early afternoon. A glass of wine or sherry is the extent of my drinking now. My iPhone does ding after I have turned off the lights, but that is usually a child or grandchild sharing a text message. I love hearing from them, so don't want them to take me off their distribution list. Perhaps I should leave the phone in another room at night?

A habit my wife and I have developed since COVID-19 made its entrance a year ago is to slip between the covers and watch a movie before letting sleep take the reins. Our preference is for light fare—the Thin Man series, with William Powell and Myrna Loy; an old Fred Astaire and Ginger Rogers musical, like *Top Hat* or *Swing Time*; or a comedy with Spencer Tracy and Katherine Hepburn, like *Desk Set* or *Adam's Rib*. Professionals advise against television in the bedroom, but it does not seem to me that old black-and-white movies emit much of the blue light that concerns them. However, there are evenings when we risk censure by watching newer detective series, like Agatha Christie's Hercule Poirot and Jane Marple, Inspector Morse (whose first name is pagan!), or Inspector Maigret. These shows include some humor and a little heart-thumping suspense. About half the time, I never make it to the end of the movie anyway. But that is the advantage of watching old favorites—one knows what one has missed, so it isn't missed!

If I want to shut out the sound of the television or my wife's questions, I roll to my left, with my bad right ear up. If feeling agreeable, I roll to the right so I can half-heartedly listen to the TV and grunt responses to my wife. E. Joseph Cossman, a one-time door-to-door salesman and mail-order entrepreneur, once wrote: "The best bridge between despair and hope is a good night's sleep." Easy to say, but harder to do when my eighty-year-old body is reliving its fifteen-year-old adolescence. Dale Carnegie advises us to get up and do something: "It's the worry that gets you, not the lack of sleep." So, I do. I get up, slip into another room and escape into a Trollope, a Wodehouse, or letters from E. B. White. My mind relaxes and my pulse rate subsides. If not reading something comforting, I might gather notes I had scribbled on a pad next to my bed and see if I can decipher what I had thought so ingenious when I wrote them in the dark.

When my head hits the pillow, my brain goes into overdrive. I think of luck, which plays a big part in all our lives. And I think of how lucky I have been, yet I have done nothing to be so blessed. I worry about COVID-19, and I worry about our government's response to it. I worry about the amount of debt our state and nation carry, especially unfunded liabilities, and what the effect will be on markets, so important to our future well-being. I worry about the claim (ahistorical and unfounded, in my opinion) that we are a nation of systemic racists, of the slide in our nation's cultural values and morals, and how our grandchildren will cope in a world that combines Orwell's *1984* with the meanness of a Senator Joseph McCarthy. I fear a "managed" economy will replace free market forces, thereby reducing everyone's standard of living. And I know there is little I can do about any of this. On other nights, a kaleidoscopic album of childhood images races through my mind, causing me to think back on shameful things I have done and hurtful words I have uttered. I think of people I have upset, and opportunities I have missed, and I think of those I once loved who are now gone. While I know I am not alone in having these thoughts, I realize that one is never so alone as when enmeshed in childhood memories.

And yet . . . perhaps you know the scene from the 1950 movie *Father of the Bride*, with Spencer Tracy and Joan Bennett, with the two of them in their separate beds. Tracy, as Stanley Banks, works himself into a lather, convinced his daughter's fiancé, Buckley Dunstan, is a crook, a swindler, perhaps even a kidnapper or murderer. With his rants, he wakes his wife. Having released his emotions he falls asleep, leaving Ellie Banks to silently stew over the concerns her husband passed on to her.

So, I feel like Stanley. Thanks for reading. I am better for getting these anxieties off my chest and will sleep soundly tonight. I hope I have not upset you.

Laundry
April 4, 2021

Maybe a good rule in life is never become too important to do your own laundry.

Barry Sanders (1968–)
Former running back, Detroit Lions

During my first seventy-five years, I never thought about what happened to dirty clothes tossed on the floor. I just knew they would reappear in a few days, cleaned, folded, and placed in a bureau drawer. When in boarding school, dirty laundry was mailed home, a foul-smelling gift to my mother. In college and in the army, memories of doing laundry have disappeared. Perhaps I never changed my clothes? Or perhaps that nightmare about a laundromat was not a dream?

Things changed when we moved to Essex Meadows. Caroline was recovering from a fractured pelvis incurred six months earlier. And I had retired from a job as a stockbroker in New York. Our laundry equipment, now a stacked washer-dryer, was stuffed into a former closet that is filled with paper towels, toilet paper, toolboxes, cleaning fluids, soap, napkins, extra food (cookies, especially), a shredder, and a spare vacuum cleaner. There might even be a grandchild left behind from a pre-pandemic visit. But I suspect not. I think we would have heard something.

At any rate, given our changed circumstances, I volunteered to be washer-person. Through trial and error, I mastered the complexities of how much and when to add detergents. I learned the drying cycle and, with my wife's verbal assistance, came to know which clothes should be dried on a line strung between two cabinets. Now healthy as a horse and with a beatific smile on her innocent face, she has domesticated me in other matters. I was disabused of the notion that meals arrive on the table without preparation and that cleaning up afterwards was performed by mysterious, ghost-like creatures. Army basic training had taught me to make my bed, but in years of rising before the sun that talent had been lost and had to be relearned.

"We should all do what, in the long run, gives us joy," wrote E. B. White, "even if it is only picking grapes or sorting laundry." Joy is not the emotion I feel when I dump the still-warm, dried clothes on the bed, preparatory to sorting. It is satisfaction in a job well done, and I like the feel and the smell. The poet and author, Kathleen Norris, has written that doing laundry, like taking a walk by oneself, is a good time for contemplation. I agree. The job is mechanical, requiring little thought, leaving room for ideas to bounce around in what is left of my brain. When poaching an egg or tucking in a disobedient bed sheet, attention must be paid, but sorting laundry can be done on autopilot. T-shirts belong with T-shirts and boxer shorts with boxer shorts. My inner Walter Mitty has my mind wander, sometimes in creative directions.

For one who anthropomorphizes all living things, from toads to skunk cabbage, who believes fairies lurk under leaves and who makes book on which ice cube will be the last to disappear down the drain, it was easy to once marvel at how dirty clothes could become clean without effort. The last five years have taught me to appreciate the effort it takes, and to better understand the job my wife once performed and which my daughter and daughters-in-law now do, along with all those who, daily, confront piles of dirty laundry.

Summer Days
June 19, 2021

In the trees the night wind stirs, bringing the leaves to life, endowing them with speech; the electric lights illuminate the green branches from the underside, translating them into a new language.

E. B. White (1899–1985)
Here is New York, 1949
Written, as White notes in his foreword, ". . . in the summer of 1948 during a hot spell."

On the eve of the summer solstice, June 21, 2008, Caroline and I, as guests of a friend, attended a black-tie benefit at the Hermitage in Saint Petersburg, one of the world's most beautiful museums. At 58.8 degrees north, there were only six hours of night, a strange sensation for someone living in Connecticut, 1,300 miles south and 4,000 miles west.

Forty-eight years earlier, in the summer of 1960, I had a summer job working with a Canadian mineral exploration company, which was owned by Thayer Lindsley (a friend of my parents) and led by Doug Wilmot, along the South Nahanni River on the border of the Yukon in Canada's Northwest Territories. We were close to the 61st Parallel, or about 850 miles north of the US–Canada border. I recall traipsing along dried-up riverbeds, carrying a pick looking for minerals, and a .30-06 Springfield rifle in case of an unfriendly Grizzly. At night, lying in my sleeping bag, I was happy that night creatures had only a few hours to make their rounds.

Two years later, on August 11, I was at Fort Dix, beginning eight weeks of basic training. The camp, which no longer functions as an army training center, sat on 6,500 acres in New Jersey's Pine Barrens. Fort Dix had been integrated eleven years earlier. By my day all recruits, regardless of race or class, were treated with equal disrespect—a necessary tactic to mold us into the soldiers we were to become. I was assigned to Company A, of the Third Training Regiment, where we were taught to become "the ultimate weapon"—an optimistic goal for a bunch of army reservists. That summer we marched along hot, dusty roads; crawled under barbwire with machine guns firing live ammunition over our heads;

trained with bayonets (which I prayed I would never have to use); bivouacked in fields; and crawled through swamps in nighttime maneuvers. There is a photo of me with two friends, Jerry (Girard) Stein and Marcel Shwergold. Cigarettes in hand, we are on a ten-minute break.

In *Travels with Charley*, John Steinbeck wrote: "What good is the warmth of summer, without the cold of winter to give it sweetness." An understandable sentiment for a child who grew up in New Hampshire. In her novel, *To Kill a Mockingbird*, with Scout speaking, Harper Lee wrote: "Summer was on the way; Jem and I awaited it with impatience. Summer was our best season: it was sleeping on the back screened porch in cots, or trying to sleep in the tree house; summer was everything good to eat. . . ." Looking back, I see my hotly anticipated summer days were full: Summer began with a Fourth of July baseball game in Wellesley where my father grew up, and it ended just before Labor Day with a trip to the East River section of Madison, Connecticut, where my mother grew up. In between, we rode horses through the woods and along dirt roads and sometimes competed in local horseshows. We swam in Nubanusit Lake, Willard Pond, and Dublin Lake, but most often in Norway Pond, which is in the center of Hancock village, four miles from our home. In the evenings, we caught fireflies, which Robert Frost said, "never equal stars in size," and inhaled the soft, sweet smells of New Hampshire's countryside. We picked blackberries on Cobb's Hill and highbush blueberries in the "next field." We ate watermelon in the backyard off a table my father had made with wire mesh, so no need to wipe it clean. Going to bed on the sleeping porch, we witnessed eerie shadows cast by trees, as moonlight fell on the "Goat Pasture."

Happy summer days

In his poem "The House Was Quiet and the World Was Calm," Wallace Stevens wrote: "The summer night is like a perfection of thought."

As I grew older, summer jobs consumed much of the daytime—working in gardens, haying, giving riding lessons, and working with construction crews. Coming home for summer vacation from boarding school, I felt like *The Great Gatsby*'s Nick Carraway with "that familiar conviction that life was beginning over again with the summer." In the evenings as I got older, we attended square dances in nearby townhalls and—four times a summer—formal dances at the Dublin Lake Club, with Lester Lanin in attendance, a strange contrast to mornings in a hayfield. In my 1947 Ford sedan (owned jointly with my sister), a friend and I would take girls to drive-in movies in Keene.

Sunday will be the start of my eighty-first summer. Memories run together. In 1995, we left Greenwich for Old Lyme (keeping a small apartment in New York). Summer weekends were spent sculling the marsh creeks along the Connecticut River's estuary; swimming, playing "at" golf and tennis, and kayaking with grandchildren. We continued to spend August in Rumson, New Jersey, where my wife had spent her childhood summers, and in the morning, I would take the six o'clock Fast Ferry into New York from the Highlands. June months of twenty-four and twenty-three years ago saw two of our children married, and during the summers of 2000, 2002, and 2008 three of our ten grandchildren were born, including the oldest and the youngest.

Looking back on all those summers, these memories are to be cherished: from childhood to summer jobs, to falling in love and then watching our children laugh, play, and grow up, and then, later, watching their children do the same. These memories bring wistful smiles on languid summer days when blue skies lure us to the fields and paths that surround where we live. We marvel at the gift nature has wrought—myriad shades of green, and the wildlife that shares this precious planet. "Summer specializes in time, slows it down almost to dream," writes Jennifer Grotz in her poem "Late Summer." The days will get shorter as August melds into September. It is preparation for the autumn, which will see much of plant and wildlife take long siestas, storing strength for the long winter and spring's renewal. In like manner, we store up memories for our fall and winter evenings. But in the meantime, we have the start of summer days.

My Token Moment
July 3, 2021

The making of friends who are real friends is the best token
we have of a man's success in life.

Edward Everett Hale (1822–1909)
The Man Without a Country

Perhaps it was my sheltered childhood, or maybe it was the time in which I grew up, but the concept of tokenism never entered my mind, even when my older sister dressed me in her clothes. I never felt singled out, though as her younger brother nearest in age, I was. I just didn't realize it. Even when standing on her bed, wearing her Mary Janes, I never saw myself as a symbol of something profound. Women, in my early life played an important role, and not just because I was my sister's plaything. With a whimsical father, my mother was the more practical. My maternal grandfather died when I was six, so my grandmother played the grandparent role for both. Of my paternal grandparents, my grandmother, an independent woman, was my grandfather's equal in all respects. Her counsel was wise. She once advised me not to marry a Mary. There were too many in the family, she said, and marry a woman older than you, as they live longer than men. Sage suggestions, which I took and never looked back.

And I never felt privileged. Maybe that was because of privilege. To the oblivious, they say, ignorance is bliss. I grew up as a white, Anglo-Saxon male in a Protestant-monopolized small New Hampshire town. While we had horses to ride and hundreds of books, the house was four miles from the village and there was no television. We slept three or four to a bedroom. My mother cooked (when she did) on a woodstove and kept milk in a real icebox. There was no central heat and, of course, no air-conditioning. The telephone was a "party line," meaning we shared it with others. The "privileged," if I thought of them that way, lived in town with a TV, electric stove, refrigerator, and a private telephone line.

While women were a strong influence in my early years, men were ever-present. As a sculptor, my father's studio was in our backyard, if we dared interrupt him. Among my siblings, I was the second oldest of five boys and four girls. While supposed to set a good example, I never did. I went to an all-boys high school and, in college, while I enjoyed the company of women, I mostly hung out with male friends. There were women soldiers when I was in the army, but Fort Dix was dominated by men, albeit of mixed races and religions. During my forty-eight years on Wall Street, I worked with all genders, races, and religions, but women and racial minorities, while present, never dominated.

Now, at Essex Meadows, I find myself in a matriarchal society, and I have a better sense of what it is to be part of a minority—at least in gender. Women residents outnumber men, roughly three to two. The CEO of this retirement community is a woman, as are six of the seven department heads. I could not be happier.

Recently, Caroline and I were invited to dinner with two charming ladies. They wanted a man, one of them said, so would we join them? For a moment my feelings were hurt. It was not my imagined scintillating wit or presumed verbal sparring prowess they wanted; it was because I was a man. It was my token moment. But if that be tokenism, I look forward to many more such moments.

Once More to Peterborough
August 3, 2021

*It is strange how much you can remember about places like that once you allow
your mind to return to grooves which lead back.*

E. B. White (1899–1985)
"Once More to the Lake," August 1941

Thomas Wolfe's posthumously published novel, *You Can't Go
Home Again*, tells the story of George Webber, a fledging author,
who frequently references his hometown in a book he is writing, to
the annoyance of the town's residents. I spent three days last week in
my hometown, with my wife and a grandson. And we did so without
annoying anyone . . . at least as far as I know.

In his essay, "Once More to the Lake," E. B. White tells the story of
taking his ten-year-old son to the lake in Maine to which his father had
brought him when he was a small boy. He writes evocatively of mortality—how each new generation replaces the former. In the last sentence he
wrote of his son pulling on a cold, wet bathing suit, a habit he remembered from his childhood: "As he buckled the swollen belt suddenly my
groin felt the chill of death."

Our Town is Thornton Wilder's 1938 play about living in Grover's
Corners, a small New Hampshire village, around the turn of the previous
century. Through the "Stage Manager," he tells of the Gibbs and Webb
families—their births, loves, and deaths. Wilder began to write the play
at Peterborough's MacDowell Colony, which makes it special to those of
us from that part of New Hampshire. It was first performed at the Peterborough Players in 1940. On this trip we ran into Beth Brown whose
grandmother, Edith Bond Stearns, started the Peterborough Players in
1933. I remember Mrs. Stearns and her daughter Sally Stearns Brown, a
friend to my parents. (Beth was the age of my younger siblings and used
to take riding lessons from my mother.) With Beth was Gordon Clapp,
the New Hampshire-born, Emmy-winning actor who will play the Stage
Manager in a revival of the play to be staged outdoors in Peterborough, in
about two weeks. (Unfortunately for us, the performance coincides with
our annual time at the Jersey shore.)

On this latest return to Peterborough, Caroline, grandson Alex Williams, and I had an "*Our Town*-like" experience. Act III of the play opens at the Grover's Corners cemetery, on "a hilltop—a windy hilltop—lots of sky, lots of clouds. . . ." We drove to Pine Hill Cemetery, which is on a hillside. Looking south from the graves of my family there was little wind but lots of sky. Wilder's cemetery held mountain laurel and lilacs. In this, nestled under white pines, rest my paternal grandparents, my parents, a brother, a sister, and an uncle and an aunt. American flags decorate my father's and uncle's graves, commemorating their service in World War II. We stop and spend a few minutes in quiet reflection. Driving out, we pass tombstones with familiar names—Bishop, Nichols, Pettengill, Snow, Wilson, and Shattuck—each conjuring a memory of an individual from my past.

The purpose of this Peterborough trip was to meet with publisher, Sarah Bauhan, and her art director, Henry James, about a book to be published next year, *Essays from Essex*. It is to be illustrated by my grandson, who brought some of his artwork, including a drawing for the cover.

We stayed at the Cranberry Meadow Farm Inn, a bed and breakfast now owned by Carolyn and Charlie Hough. It was built in 1797 as the Wilson Tavern but was converted to a private home in 1834. Again an inn, it is located about two miles from the village, on the corner of Old Street Road and Route 101. It sits on eighty acres, with wonderful walking trails. When I was a child, we would pass the house when driving home from skiing at Temple Mountain; my father mentioning that legend claimed it was a stop on the Underground Railway.

Following our meeting with Sarah, we drove past the house where I grew up on Middle Hancock Road, four miles from town and now looking sad, with weeds in the driveway and in need of paint. Gone were the cries of children happily playing, the bustling business of my parents' Red Shed Rubber Animals, the music from the radio that kept my father company in his studio, the barking of dogs, the neighing of horses, the bleating of goats, and the rattling of the male peacock's outstretched tail as he flirted with his peahen. Through the woods and over the hill, we drove by my grandparent's summer home on Windy Row, now owned by a cousin, Nathanael "Sandy" Greene. While there is a new garage, the house and grounds are well maintained and look as welcoming as they did sixty years ago.

We visited the Unitarian Church (now the Unitarian Universalist Church), which dominates the town's center. The large, historic brick

My brother, Willard, and his wife Holly
at The Toadstool in Peterborough

building is located on the corner of Main and Summer Streets. In 1956, twenty-eight-year-old David Parke was ordained at the church and served as minister for five years. He was a favorite of my father's. He returned seven years after leaving to officiate at my father's funeral in December 1968. My five youngest siblings were christened there and three of my sisters were married before its altar. Besides my father, funeral services were held in the church for my mother, a sister, and a brother. At all three, I gave eulogies.

Street layouts in the town remain much as they had been, but old stores are gone, replaced by restaurants and small specialty food, art, and clothing stores. Derby's, once the town's department store, is now an art gallery. Clukay's Pharmacy, where we bought nickel ice cream cones, is a clothing store, and the land on which sat the Village Pharmacy, owned by Myer and Florence Goldman, now sits a bank. The hardware store on Grove Street is a restaurant. The Nichols Ford Dealership, bought in the 1950s by Milt Fontaine, has moved out of the village. The American Guernsey Cattle Club building, built in 1950 and the town's largest building, now houses a variety of businesses, including Bauhan Publishing. The railroad no longer comes to town and Depot Square, where we used to meet my grandmother when she arrived on the train from Connecticut, now houses the Toadstool, my brother Willard's bookstore, the largest retail outlet in the village. Shopping centers have sprung up outside of town, on land which was once fields and woods.

Thomas Wolfe was correct: You can never relive the life you once knew. But we can recall past times. In returning to Peterborough, I am reminded of scenes from long ago—stopping at a diner in Brattleboro after a day's skiing at Hogback; picking blackberries on Cobb's Hill, galloping along dirt roads, swimming in Norway Pond; arguing with my father at the dining room table; listening to my mother as she read aloud a Jane Austen novel; taking a long walk with David Parke, when he recommended *Only Yesterday* by Frederick Lewis Allen, a history of the 1920s. In turn, I recommended the book to my author daughter-in-law, Beatriz Williams, who tells me it was important to her understanding of that decade.

As we age, there is in us a bid for immortality, a desire to recapture our youth—to go home again. But that is an impossible dream. But it is possible and healthy to revisit venues of our past, and to recall people and places that shaped who we have become. And when we are gone, we hope our children and grandchildren will do the same, so that our bid for immortality comes true, at least in their memories.

Essex Meadows—Our New Home
March 10, 2016

You can't help getting older, but you don't have to get old.

George Burns (1896–1996)

When my wife and I moved to Old Lyme twenty-five years ago we were still young enough to consider ourselves immortal; the end game was something over the horizon. Now that we are older, we know the track does not extend forever. But we don't let that influence how we live. We believe in Eleanor Roosevelt's maxim: "Life [is] meant to be lived and curiosity must be kept alive."

Moving, it has been said, is one of the more traumatic events in one's life. It has not been foreign to us. It's not that we are peripatetic, but neither have we always lived in one place. We had moved to Greenwich in 1971, seven years after we were married, with a complement of three children. (The youngest, Edward, had been born a few weeks before we departed the rural Connecticut town of Durham for the sophistication of Greenwich.) Twenty-four years later we moved from that high-maintenance, fast-paced suburb, where we had raised our children, to the somnambulant, shoreline town of Old Lyme. We had been happy in Greenwich, but the town was evolving and so were we. We sold our house on Lake Avenue, rented a small pied-à-terre in New York, and made Old Lyme our home.

The years went by. In time, we (principally that meant me) spent less time in New York and more in Old Lyme. I was writing more and "stockbrokering" less. There was less need for me to be in the city. The house in Old Lyme, with its river, marshes, gardens, and the community and friends played big roles in our lives. Seductively, they drew us in. Old Lyme is, and has been for 120 years, an art colony noted for American Impressionists. The colony was begun by Henry Ward Ranger in 1899. He brought with him artists like Willard Metcalf, Carleton Wiggins, Clark Voorhees, George Bruestle, Everett Warner, Frank Bicknell, and Childe Hassam. They took rooms in the home of Florence Griswold, the penurious widow of a sea captain. Woodrow Wilson, then president of Princeton University, spent the summer of 1910 at the colony, because his wife, Ellen Axson Wilson, wanted to paint with Old Lyme artists. (Wilson would be elected New Jersey's governor that fall.) The town's bucolic scenery lured more than just painters. The Connecticut River estuary attracted Roger Tory Peterson, naturalist, ornithologist, and artist. He made his home for over forty years on the banks of Old Lyme's Lieutenant River. Jim Calhoun, Hall of Fame basketball coach, began his career as basketball coach at Lyme–Old Lyme High School. Albert Einstein spent several summers in the village.

A year and a half ago, we decided another move was in the cards. "Tidelands," as our place was called, was becoming too much for us. It was beautiful, but we wanted to be masters of our future, not servants to our house and land. We recognized that the strings that comprise the cycle of life have beginnings and endings. We are born and grow up. We become adults. We marry and have children. The children grow up and become young adults; they marry, have children of their own, and we become grandparents. Time, like Ol' Man River, keeps rolling along. We were getting older, but didn't want to "get old," as George Burns said.

We had known about Essex Meadows almost from the time we moved to Old Lyme. It had opened three years before we bought our house. When it was suggested, as it was early on, that we purchase an apartment to ensure the well-being of our "golden" years, we joined the chorus of those who irreverently referred to the place as "Exit Meadows"—God's waiting room, a place to go for one's last supper, or, at least, one's last few years. It was not for the young and virile, as we saw ourselves. A better idea, we thought, was to move to a cottage in the village.

However, as a consequence of a fall Caroline took last July Fourth, our thinking changed. Caroline spent four weeks in the health center of Essex Meadows. It was not, we learned, a place where people went when all hope had disappeared. The center was intent on curing patients and sending them home. The facility was clean and pleasant, the staff professional and welcoming. So, instead of moving to a place from which we might be forced to leave because of infirmities or ill-health—a move that then might well be engineered by our children rather than ourselves— why not move to an apartment in the Essex Meadows complex and make it a home we could enjoy and be happy in?

Essex Meadows is a "life-care retirement community." It is a family-owned business, managed by LifeCare Services, LLC. "EM," as it is known,

Golf course at Essex Meadows

is a community of 182 apartments, thirteen cottages, and a forty-bed health center. In all, there are about 240 residents, with a staff of a hundred. Over the past decade the average age of new residents has declined from the mid-eighties to the high seventies. There is a fitness room, swimming pool, and trails through the surrounding woods. The 108 acres on which Essex Meadows was built abuts what is known locally as The Preserve, which consists of 1,000 acres of protected land that falls within the towns of Essex, Old Saybrook, and Westbrook. It is the largest undeveloped coastal parcel between Boston and New York. (In part, The Preserve owes its existence to the 2008 bankruptcy of Lehman Brothers, but that is a story for another time.) Given the relatively small size of Essex Meadows and the friendliness of its residents and staff, it feels more like a club than a "life-care" community. While there are bridge games, shuffle-board competitions, swimming aerobics, discussion groups, documentaries, movies, and trips to museums, Essex Meadows emphasizes that moving here is a change of address, not a change in lifestyle. What you do is up to you.

Essex, with its boatyards, the Griswold Inn, yacht clubs, and a few boutiques, was recently ranked number one among the "100 Best Small Towns in America." The town is across the Connecticut River and about five miles up from Old Lyme. It is a beautiful and historic village, with an obvious emphasis on boating, particularly sailing. Whereas Old Lyme is a "beach" town, Essex is defined by the river. The village juts, like a thumb, east into the Connecticut between North and South Coves. In the early years of the United States, Essex was a principal boatbuilding place, including ships for the young nation's fledgling navy. During the War of 1812, on the night of April 8, 1814, the British rowed up the river from Old Saybrook and burned twenty-seven ships in Essex Harbor. It is said that this event did more than anything else to rally Americans to defeat the British. The war ended with the British acceptance of terms laid out in Ghent in late December 1814. (The Battle of New Orleans—a decisive victory by the American forces—took place in January 1815, after the war was over but before the signed Treaty arrived in Washington.)

"Why," my wife's brother asked when he heard we were moving to Essex Meadows, "would you want to move to a nursing home?" Apart from the sarcasm implied in the question, his words denote a common misunderstanding. Communities like this are relatively new. Throughout most of history, children cared for aging parents, despite the fact that people age more like a bad cheese than a good wine. The wealthy, of course, could afford in-home care, but the majority relied on family. Nursing homes were first on the scene, but often those were dismal, odoriferous reminders of the unpleasantness of getting older. Continuing-care facilities were designed to be pleasant places in which to live. They eased the burden otherwise foisted on one's children, and mitigated costs and inconveniences. Early on, people moved to facilities like Essex Meadows when the ability to care for oneself had become difficult. Essex Meadows is, as their advertising claims, a change of address.

Being younger than most living here, my wife and I wanted to ensure our independence. We see ourselves as living in an apartment, with pleasant neighbors. I can write, as I always have. But we can easily turn off the lights, shut the door, and visit our grandchildren or travel wherever we wish. In time, we may well choose to participate in more of Essex Meadows' activities, but not for the moment.

Once the decision was made, we remodeled the apartment—including changing the floors and ceilings. We did this at our expense. We added moldings and built-ins. We created a library/office. We upgraded the bathrooms and kitchen and installed a laundry room. We improved the quality of the interior doors and lighting fixtures. In doing so, we added to our emotional well-being, while knowing the money spent would not be recovered. Like most institutions of this type, one "buys in" by purchasing a unit—some percentage of which is returned to the person (or to his or her estate) when they leave. The balance, along with the monthly charge, offsets costs incurred.

But what we have is a beautiful home. The oriental carpets are ones we brought from Old Lyme and the furniture, a mixture of antiques and family pieces, fits in. On the walls hang more than 130 paintings, etchings, prints, and photographs, all of which we have had for years. Other photos, mementos, and artwork adorn tables and chests.

As I peck at my computer, Caroline, our children, and grandchildren surround me. In one photo, my artist parents call to one another through the ears of a self-sculpted snow face. In another sit my four sisters, while a third has me standing with my four brothers. My maternal grandfather Hotchkiss, pipe in hand, perches on my desk. My grandfather Williams, working at his desk while I do at mine, looks down from the wall. In one photograph, I sit squirming on the lap of my great-grandmother Washington. Another has me in a rowboat with my sister, Mary, brother, Frank, two cousins, and both grandfathers. There is a photo of four generations: my father, his mother, me, and year-old son Sydney. There is a fading Polaroid print, taken by Dr. Land, of me and my friend, Duncan Kendall. We look like the wise-asses we were at age sixteen. Framed ancestral letters adorn one wall, along with photographs. Caroline has similar photos of her childhood and family. Examples of my parents' sculpture can be seen throughout the apartment. On the walls are hung artwork: Old Lyme impressionists; other paintings, prints, and etchings; a portrait of Caroline and another of my mother. There are two paintings Caroline did when in college, a painting done by grandson Alex, and drawings by my parents. These photos, paintings, and ephemera of family and friends evoke memories that are personal. They bring color to the past; they help guide us toward the future; they represent that which cannot be taken from us.

We knew we had been successful when our granddaughter, Emma, first saw the apartment: "It looks just like Old Lyme," she exclaimed as she walked through the door. The colors of the walls, the paintings, and furniture looked familiar. She meant, I believe, that it looked like home. Maya Angelou once said, "The ache for home lives in all of us, the safe place where we can go as we are and not be questioned." That is what we have found at Essex Meadows. It may not work for everyone, but it is home to us.

Mentoring
June 14, 2017

A mentor is someone who sees more talent and ability within you, than you see in yourself and helps bring it out of you.

Bob Proctor
Canadian author, speaker, and mentor

While campaigning in Virginia in 2008, President Obama said, "If you've got a business—you didn't build that. Somebody else made that happen." Later, in the same speech, he did mention the need for individual initiative. While Mr. Obama stated his belief that government is instrumental in individual success, he was also referring to the role mentors play.

A mentorship can be defined as a relationship in which a more experienced or more knowledgeable, usually older person helps guide a less experienced, usually younger person. People who do well in school and in sports often attribute their success to the dedication of a teacher or coach. The same can be said for those beginning careers, and it is true even for old goats who, late in life, take up writing essays. Mentors help turn doubt into determination, aspiration into accomplishment. Earlier this year, in the *Harvard Business Review*, Anthony Tjan wrote that "mentors need to be givers of energy, not takers of it."

Mentoring is a way of giving back. Five years ago, I was invited to join a small group of retirees in Old Lyme, people who realized their experiences and talents could be of use to others. While I was not then retired, I was spending most Fridays in the country, so Friday morning meetings worked. We called ourselves Mentoring Corps for Community Development (MCCD), a 501(c)3 organization. Our website speaks to the "sparkle" we try to add to our town and the region—Old Lyme and southeastern Connecticut. Over the years, we have worked with schools and students, with families who have experienced natural disasters, and individuals who have suffered hardships. We have aided nonprofit organizations and helped small businesses. We try to abide by advice Robert Frost once gave: "I am not a teacher, but an awakener."

We all have had mentors in one form or another. Mistakes are a form of mentoring. Certainly, that has been true for me. While I was not smart enough to learn from them all, I have learned from some: my rudeness, when I was fourteen, to a young girl who was not very popular; a wise man who gently advised my sixteen-year-old self about the risks of speeding on back roads; a group of construction types who separated me from my paycheck when I was seventeen; I learn from my grandchildren who chide me when I mess up.

But I also benefitted from those who mentored me: a teacher of English at Williston Academy, Horace "Thugsy" Thorner, whose class on *Macbeth* and *Hamlet* I have never forgotten; an instructor in journalism in college; and the editor of *Foster's Daily Democrat* in Dover, New Hampshire, for whom I wrote a sports column. I recall being told by my first real boss—Jim Donnelly of Eastman Kodak—that, if I set my mind to it, I could achieve anything. I was taught the basics of selling equities to institutional investors by Andy Monness, who thirty years later encouraged my fledging writing career. He often disagreed with my opinions but liked the way I expressed them. As important as anything, in terms of my writing, have been the hundreds like you who have corrected me when I was in error, challenged my opinions when yours differed, and emboldened me in offering praise, not all of it deserved. I consider you all mentors.

It is when we are young, and not fully formed, that mentorship is most effective. I think of an experience in mid-summer 1960. I was a member of a prospecting team in the Northwest Territories of Canada, along the Nahanni River. It was 3,000 miles from home and about two hundred miles from a village, not to mention a road. I was nineteen and lonely. There were twenty people in the expedition, most of whom were at least twenty years my senior. In mid-July, we were to move the base camp about one hundred miles further north. I told the manager, Doug Wilmot, that I wanted to go home. He said fine, just help us move the camp. He said nothing more. A week later, once the camp was moved, we prospectors were ordered back to the field. I joined the others without hesitation. I have always been thankful I did. Quitting would have been something I would have regretted the rest of my life. I am grateful that Mr. Wilmot handled me as he did—no arguments, no recriminations, no attempts to convince me of the error I would have made by leaving betimes, and no smugness at my decision to stay.

When thinking of mentoring, we typically think of bright, talented, but reserved or introverted students who come to the attention of an observant, caring, and capable teacher. A January 2014 report titled "The Mentoring Effect," commissioned by the National Mentoring Partnership, found significant positive outcomes for those who had a mentor: They were more likely to aspire to or attend college; they were more likely to participate in sports or extracurricular activities; they were more likely to assume leadership roles in school, and more likely to volunteer in their communities. While the political focus is on funding underperforming schools, the greater need is finding teachers, coaches, and volunteers who will give counsel and care to students navigating the shoals that separate childhood from adulthood. Benjamin Franklin once wrote, "Tell me and I forget. Teach me and I may remember. Involve me and I learn."

But, as important as mentoring is, it is no guarantor of success. It is not a magic elixir. It cannot substitute for a lack of aspiration and initiative. It cannot compensate for those who do not work hard, or who do not show fortitude. We all know the adage of leading a horse to water. Mentees, like Dickens' Barkis, must be "willing." Good mentors, as Mr. Proctor notes in the rubric at the start of this essay, see a spark that just needs igniting. Two thousand years ago, Plutarch wrote, as a lesson to both mentors and mentees, "The mind is not a vessel to be filled, but a fire to be kindled."

Looking back on my life, I count myself lucky—fortunate to have been born into the family I was, and lucky to have been born at the time I was. I was fortunate in the woman who agreed to be my wife, in our children, and now in our grandchildren. I have been fortunate in my friends, both new and old. I was lucky to have served in the military when I did, after Korea and (just) before Vietnam. I was fortunate to have a career and a job that I loved. I have been lucky in my health, and thankful I was blessed to find an avocation as a writer. I was favored to have been endowed with an optimistic outlook. And I was fortunate to have had help from so many people over the years.

And now, as age creeps up and I think of the past seven decades, I am thankful I can give back something through MCCD. Mentoring is partial payment for all I have received.

LITERATURE

This last section on literature is comprised of eight essays, not all having to do with literature. In fact, "The Messy Desk" snuck into this section because there was no other place to put it. A clean desk, it is claimed by some, "suggests generosity and conventionality." I like to think of myself as generous, and I hope I am not conventional. A messy desk is supposed to reflect creativity. As for that, I will leave you, the reader, to be the judge. There are two essays on writing, which, coming from an amateur, may be a bit of a stretch.

An Essay on Writing Essays
May 18, 2016

Nothing is so firmly believed as that which we least know.

Michel de Montaigne (1533–1592)
The Essays of Michel de Montaigne, 1580

A blank Word document stares out from the computer screen. I sit before it—the essayist at work? No one sits down to write without some idea—perhaps muddled—of what to say. A working title is affixed, along with a date that often proves optimistic; a rubric is added. The latter helps focus wandering minds. The concept, at this early stage, assumes the shape of a globule of mercury or a tube of Silly Putty. Sculpting tangled ideas into something concise and readable requires choosing the right words, having them mean what they were meant to mean. Essayists don't have the latitude of Humpty Dumpty: "When I use a word, it means just what I choose it to mean—neither more nor less." Our words must be understood.

Writers of essays don't want to leave readers puzzled like Alice. Obfuscation is the province of politicians, not essayists. The purpose of the latter is to make thoughts intelligible, as they get transported from mind to paper to mind. (Politicians hope their words appeal to those who read carelessly and listen inattentively.)

Periods, colons, semicolons, commas, dashes, and parentheses are not there to look pretty, but to add clarity. Even the lowly apostrophe is defended by the Apostrophe Protection Society! Lynne Truss wrote in *Eats, Shoots & Leaves*, that punctuation is "the basting that holds the fabric of language in shape." Edward Estlin Cummings, better known as e e cummings, chose to write poetry in lowercase letters and without punctuation. He was an artist. We are mechanics, not dilettantish virtuosos who obscure the meaning of what they write. We are more like photographers than contemporary artists. What we write should not be left to the reader's interpretation.

The word essay derives from the French *essai*, which means to attempt. It was first used by Michel de Montaigne, the man generally considered the father of the modern essay. Montaigne was an educated nobleman who retired to his family's castle in Bordeaux at the age of thirty-two to "draw his portrait with his pen." He was a young man who knew his priorities. He once said, "For the intimate companionship of my table I choose the agreeable, not the wise. In my bed, beauty comes before virtue." All essayists write about themselves—their experiences or their ideas. "Know Thyself" was inscribed on the Temple of Apollo in Delphi. Socrates, Henry David Thoreau, Spinoza, Oscar Wilde, and the Canadian recording artist Drake, all believed that knowing oneself was crucial to a happy life.

Thus, essays reflect the writer. E. B. White, perhaps the greatest essayist of the past one hundred years, wrote in the forward to *Essays of E. B. White*: "The essayist is a self-liberated man, sustained by the childish belief that everything he thinks about, everything that happens to him, is of general interest. . . . Only a person who is congenitally self-centered has the effrontery and stamina to write essays." Joseph Epstein, in his introduction to *Windsprints,* writes that he sides with those essayists who feel "a desolating sense of uselessness if a few days go by without their writing. . . ." Almost all writers of this genre take pleasure in their craft and inject humor where possible. In the late Christopher Hitchens' posthumously published book of essays, *And Yet . . .*, there are included three hilarious and self-deprecating essays, "On the Limits of Self-Improvement, Parts I, II and III." In Part III, he writes, ". . . and the awful thing about growing older is that you begin to notice how every day consists of more and more subtracted from less and less."

Caveat emptor should be applied whenever reading political op-eds or essays. Statistics can be skewed to fit one's preconceptions. Conclusions are usually biased, based on a personal interpretation of facts. In short, they are opinions, often on subjects with which we who write have limited knowledge, as de Montaigne noted in the rubric that heads this essay. Like the non sequiturs from a dinner party guest, they are meant to startle, to start a conversation, or stimulate controversy. There are some superb writers of this type today: Jonathon Goldberg, Ross Douthat, Mary Anastasia O'Grady, Peggy Noonan, Jason Riley, Daniel Henninger, and David Brooks are but a small selection. They write well. They write, as E. B. White admonished all writers of children's literature, up not down. A few scribes, like P. J. O'Rourke and Mark Steyn, use wit and humor. And of course, there are those who use the form to show off their knowledge, even when they lack judgment.

I came late to the craft, with no training other than a love of reading. My bible has long been *The Elements of Style*, originally written by Cornell professor, William Strunk Jr. in 1920 and revised by E. B. White in 1959. The eighteen rules of composition, like Rule 10, "Use the Active Voice" and Rule 13, "Omit Needless Words," are engraved on my forehead.

My essays fall into two categories. The first have to do with subjects like politics, the economy, education, and climate. I write from my own perspective, expressing opinions, based on study and reflection. At times, the result is a wrestling match, with me wearing both the black and the white trunks. Other times, I am incensed by the stupidity that enshrouds our political and educational institutions, or by the blindness of reporters and commentators. When I see commonsense give way to political correctness, or I see universal values that have helped people live civilly for generations, be abandoned, I lose control of my pen.

The other type of essay I write is of a more personal nature—stories of my family, of growing up, of books, hiking, skiing, and kayaking, commentary on marshes, places I love. Inspiration usually arrives unexpectedly. Curiously, the longer I have been writing—and I have now written over a thousand essays—the more time each piece takes. I write in bursts, and then must spend several hours editing and rewriting. Even when I push "Send", I know that one more read-through would result in more changes—the elimination of even more needless words. For five and a half years I have been writing a third category of essays—reviews of books I have enjoyed.

An essayist is not a rhetorician. Good writing should be convincing but should not be confused with arguing persuasively. We are not lawyers. And there is no need to shout. One hopes that one's arguments, if simply and clearly stated, will persuade the reader that any comparison to dunces is purely coincidental. Keeping in mind the derivation of the word essayist, I "try" to figure things out. I am not an academic. I am no grammarian. I simply ask my sentences to say what I want them to mean. I am neither an epistemologist nor a metaphysician. In fact, I would have difficulty defining those words. People have used plenty of adjectives to describe me—many of them unprintable—but erudite has never been one. The definition of erudition that I prefer is the one used by Ambrose Bierce in his incomparable *The Devil's Dictionary*: "A noun: Dust shaken out of a book into an empty skull." Too much information, just as too much self-analysis, renders simple concepts so complex that explaining them gets lost in a jumble of incoherence. "The better the writing the less abstruse it is," advised Evelyn Waugh, in a letter to American author Thomas Merton in 1948.

Montaigne's great discovery, as noted by Paul Graham in 2004, in his essay "The Age of the Essay," was: "Expressing ideas helps to form them." Graham added, "In a real essay you're writing for yourself. You're thinking out loud." Similarly, the historian and biographer David Burton once wrote about Theodore Roosevelt that ". . . he would often write an article or essay having no immediate purpose other than to organize his thoughts." We who enjoy grappling with ideas are in good company. But essays are more than a stream of the subconscious. An audience is wanted, which means the writing must be appealing.

My first attempt at writing was in March 2000. I was a stockbroker—and had been for thirty-three years—who did not understand what was happening to the market. Absurd valuations were being given to companies with no earnings and, in some cases, with no revenues. I began tentatively, gradually becoming more assertive. I wrote what I called "Market Notes." I enjoyed the craft, as it forced me to think through issues. Eight years later, as the financial crisis descended, I started what I called "Thought of the Day," largely as a means of self-preservation. Early on, those pieces did come out once a day. But the crisis abated, and my brain grew older and more tired. I backed off to twice a week, and now once a week, or less.

In retirement, writing provides pleasure. It keeps me out of trouble—I am less of a nuisance to my wife. I hear often from well-wishers, both those I have known for years and from those I have only just met. I appreciate the accolades from those whose beliefs are similar to mine, and I enjoy sparring with friends who cannot believe my obtuseness. In a world addicted to the short term, I find writing essays allows the luxury of thinking about the long term. With age comes perspective, some elements of tolerance and, dare I say, smatterings of wisdom? I listen to criticism, sometimes absorb it, and other times chuck it. I expect to continue to write, motivated by ideas, hoping to promote discussion . . . but always with a desire to write ever better.

In *How to Tell a Story and Other Essays*, Mark Twain wrote: "Anybody can have ideas—the difficulty is to express them without squandering a quire of paper on an idea that ought to be reduced to one glittering paragraph." I like what E. B. White told George Plimpton in a 1969 interview in the *Paris Review*. "A writer should concern himself with whatever absorbs his fancy, stirs his heart, and unlimbers his typewriter . . . a writer has the duty to be good, not lousy; true, not false; lively, not dull; accurate, not full of error. He should tend to lift them up, not lower them down. Writers do not merely reflect and interpret life; they inform and shape life."

Those are high standards. Whether I have succeeded, I do not know. No need to answer, because regardless of the response, I will labor on, putting pen to paper (or fingers to keyboard), working to improve my craft.

The Messy Desk
November 23, 2016

Disorderly environments seem to inspire breaking free of tradition.

Kathleen D. Vohs
Behavioral scientist, University of Minnesota
Study published August 2013 in *Psychological Science*

I appreciate order. It would not describe me, yet it is something I learned early. Growing up, I shared a room with three siblings. When one's clothes and treasures are confined to two drawers in a bureau and a top bunk, order is necessary. The command, "Clean up your room!" was never given to me alone.

We are told that cleanliness is next to godliness. We are conditioned to believe that neatness and order are "good," and that messiness is "bad." "We are charmed by neatness," wrote Ovid. Minimalism is the guideline in art, music, and architecture. Antiques and collectibles have been consigned to the attic or the thrift shop. "Brown" furniture is out of fashion. As for pets, Cockapoos and Double Doodles have replaced the mutts of my youth. The cat, distant toward man, is fond of neatness; whereas the dog, which gives unconditional love, will roll in whatever smells the foulest. Dog pets have become toys, groomed and supervised.

Detritus comes with one interested in books—newspapers, magazines, and writing pile up. In January, Caroline and I moved to an apartment about one-third the size of our former house. Now that I share a library/office with my wife, I find confinement confining—or, at least, challenging. I try to keep in mind advice given me years ago by a friend who worked at IBM: "If you have a file on your desk that you have not looked at for six months, throw it out." But like most good advice generously proffered, it is ignored, at least by me.

In my case, chaos reigns. Under the desk are a dozen folders—subjects on which I plan to write . . . someday. Additionally, there are reams of yellow-lined pads, manila folders, and other litter. Bookshelves are jammed, intermixed with rubber animals my parents produced in the 1950s and sold to school systems around the world. There are carved wooden figures, cast iron and porcelain figurines, and approximately

My desk in Essex

seven hundred books—special books we brought with us. In our new library, forty-two framed pictures and photographs adorn what free wall space we have. When one moves from a large library to a small one, one never downsizes appropriately.

On my built-in, glass-topped desk sit many objects, some practical, but most curios that snuck in and stayed. Beneath the glass lie twenty-one pictures and photographs, one of which is a Polaroid of me and a friend, taken about 1956 by Dr. Edwin Land, who was then a summer resident of Peterborough, New Hampshire, where I grew up. My friend and I look like the arrogant wise guys we were. Another is of Caroline shortly before we met in late 1961. She looks happy, unaware that her life would change in the next few months.

Among the items on top of my desk are many that are commonly found: computer, pens, a container of paperclips, more photographs—nine, in all—a lamp, telephone, books (sixteen at last count), and scribbled notes, some illegible. There are knickknacks, which include three of my parents' rubber animals; a snuff holder carved from a whale's tooth; two cast iron, spring-loaded, non-politically correct piggy banks; quarterly tax reminders; a pair of silver dice given to me forty-five years ago by a friend who had just begun work at International Silver; two metal plates from which my mother made Christmas cards; and at least a dozen other objects, some of which lie hidden behind and beneath news clippings, magazines, and printed reports.

Above my desk, and below two rows of shelves, hang three small oil paintings and two photographs—one of me and my sister, taken in 1943 in East River, Connecticut, next to the '38 Chevy that would return us to New Hampshire. The photo shows a goat peering out the backseat rear window. He (or she) will return with us (see page 153). The other is a photograph of my parents in East River, each peering into opposite ears of a giant snow head that only young sculptors could have created. There is a framed arrowhead I found at my maternal grandmother's home in Tennessee. Everything is personal and all have meaning.

A recent article in the Life & Arts section of the *Financial Times* was titled "Say yes to the mess." Tim Harford, the article's author, begins and ends with stories of Benjamin Franklin who claimed order was necessary to be productive: "Let all your things have their places; let each part of your business have its time." Yet brilliant and exceptionally busy Franklin was messy but "in an orderly way." There are people who believe that simply being busy ensures productivity. Not Franklin. As Mr. Harford writes, "Franklin was too busy inventing bifocals and catching lightning to get around to tidying up his life. If he had worked in a deli, you can bet he wouldn't have been organizing sandwich orders. He would have been making sandwiches."

On September 22, 2013, *The New York Times* published an article about a series of studies conducted by Professor Kathleen Vohs (quoted at the start of this essay) and her staff at the University of Minnesota. It seemed to contradict the broken-windows theory that suggests disorder and neglect encourage nihilism, that chaos begets chaos. One hundred and eighty-eight people were invited into either a clean or a messy room where they spent ten minutes doing some unrelated chore, like imagining new uses for ping-pong balls. When leaving, they were presented with one of two food items, and they were asked a few questions, on topics like donating to charity. The study found that those with the cluttered desk were more creative in finding uses for ping-pong balls but tended to be less charitable and less healthy in their food choices. Those in the tidy room, while less creative, were more likely to select the apple over the

204 | WILLIAMS ∾ ESSAYS FROM ESSEX

chocolate bar. "Disorderly environments seem to inspire breaking free of tradition," concluded Dr. Vohs. However, the study also found that those who are more organized typically ate better and lived longer. I take satisfaction, though, in knowing we live in a gray world, where there are always exceptions. Living amidst clutter, I try to stay active, eat health-ily—not always successfully—and to be as charitable as I can. And I do believe in the broken-windows theory—that order begets order.

The study showed that we are influenced by our surroundings. But intrinsically we are either messy or neat. Would not Felix Unger have straightened up the messy desk? Would not Oscar Madison have trashed the neat desk? We create our surroundings. Either we use file drawers, or we pile papers on the floor.

Is my desk messy? Most people would say, of course. I do have a file cabinet and four drawers. In the latter lie important stuff, like a magni-fying glass, a flashlight, pens, some daguerreotypes of great- and great-great-grandparents, scissors, a stapler, and, naturally, more rubber ani-mals. But there is a difference between messy and disorganized. I usually can find what I need, and if it takes a little longer than it should, well I have enjoyed the nostalgic trip down memory lane. I take comfort in Albert Einstein's famous quip: "If a cluttered desk is a sign of a cluttered mind, of what, then, is an empty desk a sign?"

On Reading
February 20, 2017

The more you read, the more things you will know.
The more that you learn, the more places you'll go.

Theodor (Dr. Seuss) Geisel (1904–1991)
I Can Read with My Eyes Shut

With eyes focused on the ceiling, having been accused that what he had drunk could fill half the room, Winston Churchill allegedly retorted, "so much to do, so little time." I look at my shelves of unread books and feel the same.

Between five and ten million books have been published in my lifetime. A reasonable estimate for the number of books published before I was born would be another million, including, of course, the Bible and most of what we consider the classics: Homer, Shakespeare, Sir Walter Scott, Austen, the Brontë sisters, Dickens, Robert Louis Stevenson, Tolstoy, Dostoevsky, Melville, Hawthorne, Twain, Alcott—an array of literature that would be virtually impossible for the average person to read in a lifetime—and which would leave no time for modern fiction, poetry, essays, histories, and biographies. Thoreau once wrote, apropos of the myriad choices we are given, "Read the best books first, or you may not have a chance to read them at all." P. J. O'Rourke saw humor in the problem: "Always read something that will make you look good if you die in the middle of it."

A fast reader might plow through one hundred books a year. (I usually read between twenty-five and thirty.) But let's assume a man or woman in their eighties reads fifty books a year for seventy years. That would mean a lifetime of reading would consume 3,500 books. I am told, in this day when books come off presses like rabbits, that about 250,000 books are published each year in the United States, with another 700,000 self-published. This trend is not new. Over a century ago Oscar Wilde, placing wit to words, wrote, "In old days, books were written by men of letters and read by the public. Nowadays, books are written by the public and read by nobody." Most books, like old soldiers, fade away, leaving not even a small indentation on the mind of the reading public. My brother who owns the Toadstool (three bookstores in southern New Hampshire) tells me that perhaps a hundred or so books make *The New York Times* bestseller list every year; even then, many are bought to be displayed, not read. We are reminded of Churchill's comments on drinking: So much to read, so little time!

Like many, my eyes are bigger than my stomach. Books are purchased faster than can be read. So, the decision of which book to read is difficult. (Keep in mind, I am only capable of reading about 0.0002 percent of the books published each year, and that assumes I read nothing that was published in past years.) C. S. Lewis admonished us: "It is a good rule after reading a new book, never to allow yourself another new one [until] you have read an old one in between." Wise advice.

In general, I prefer dead writers of fiction and live writers of history and biography. There are exceptions, like my very much alive daughter-in-law, the *Times* best-selling author Beatriz Williams. Besides raising four children and keeping her husband in check, she writes two books a year. As to whether the writer is alive or dead, I am indifferent when it comes to essays. I like the deceased Michel de Montaigne, E. B. White, and Christopher Hitchens, as well as the living Joseph Epstein and Willard Spiegelman. I don't read much poetry, as I am untutored in the subject. And I have an aversion to those who skillfully (though not subtly) impose their political preferences on an unwitting reader, like ex-politicians and news anchors.

I always find it amusing that authors, when interviewed for the *Sunday New York Times Book Review*, mention that their bedside tables hold a half-dozen books. Mine has a dozen, ranging from *Earning the Rockies* by Robert Kaplan to Jane Austen's *Sense and Sensibility*. There are another thirty sitting on my desk waiting to be picked up: Kafka's *The Castle* and Edward O. Wilson's *The Origins of Creativity* square off against *Grit* and *A World in Disarray*, by Angela Duckworth and Richard Haass, respectively. While not assigning anthropomorphic qualities to books, I nevertheless believe that each fights for attention.

Sometimes a book jumps to the head of the line. That happened recently when a brother suggested *Sugar in the Blood* by Andrea Stuart—a history of Ms. Stuart's mixed-race heritage, in which she traces her roots back four hundred years, to both owners and slaves on a Barbados sugar plantation.

As one ages, time rushes by. Like most, my reading is not confined to books. Because of my weekly essays, I try to stay current on news; so, it's five newspapers a day. (If there were one paper that was truly unbiased my job would be simpler!) I also get sent essays and articles, most of which I peruse. And I try to stay reasonably up to date regarding two not-for-profit boards on which I serve. Besides, I have a wife, three children with spouses, and ten grandchildren, all of whom I love and who deserve more attention than I give them. There are other distractions: crossword puzzles; lunches and dinners with friends; and the woods near our new home which beckon; I find walking through them provides a modicum of exercise and clears up unwanted but ever-present cranial cobwebs. I need eight hours of sleep. Time is short. What gets omitted are television and, to my wife's dismay, movies. As for the latter, I periodically succumb and am almost always glad when I do.

One should always have a horde of easy-reading books—like comfort food, only for the mind. In that category, I place Wodehouse, along with mysteries by Rex Stout, Agatha Christie, Beverly Nichols, and two or three local (to this part of Connecticut) writers of mysteries: David Handler, James Benn, and Ann Blair Kloman. The latter's heroine is nice little old lady, Isobel, who, in order to live the life to which she was accustomed before her husband died, has become a contract killer . . . but only to put away those who are truly evil!

Even though my shelf space, since moving, has shrunk, it is books made with paper that attract me. I have tried electronic books, and I know that for many they are useful. For some, it is the ability to adjust the print size; for others, it is the convenience of carrying a library on a tabloid. But I like the feel of a book and the turning of pages. In recent years, I have taken to paperbacks, as I find my ability to recall is better when I underline particular passages. Remembering what one has read is therapeutic. I recall when my grandmother could no longer read, she used to recite poetry, poems she had learned as a young girl.

Reading is individual and endlessly educational. The late critic Edmund Wilson wrote, "No two persons ever read the same book." He's right. A reader inevitably places what he reads in a context with which he (or she) is familiar. Dr. Seuss saw the wisdom in reading. It is not just for entertainment—though that is important—but to get understanding: "The more that you learn, the more places you'll go."

The Writing of Memoirs
February 27, 2018

A memoir isn't a summary of a life; it's a window into a life.

William Zinsser (1922–2015)
On Writing Well, 1976

Not long ago, I was asked to speak on the subject of memoir writing. I complied, but it was a little like asking President Trump to speak on diplomacy—inexperience did not proscribe a willingness to express opinions. Memoirs expose who we are, at least if we are honest.

As we age, the past is more with us, bringing memories of youth—a time when the future was filled with prospects of playing for the Yankees, skiing the Matterhorn, or living in a castle. We think of people who formed us—parents, grandparents, teachers, siblings, cousins, friends, neighbors, spouses, children—and we remember places and experiences—schools, colleges, and sports, first trips alone, first jobs, marriage. We think of the role chance plays in our lives, mistakes we made, losses we endured and of victories and successes we had. Getting older makes us consider a time when we will no longer be here. How will we be remembered? What will be our legacy? Memoirs are one answer.

A memoir serves as a bridge, between the past we knew and the future that is for others. There is no better way for the young to understand the past than to learn from those who lived it. A reading of history provides facts and chronology, but memoirs provide the details that make history come alive. They are, as Mr. Zinsser wrote in the rubric quoted above, the "window into a life." They are not the magical door to C. S. Lewis' Narnia. They make a past we have lived become real to future generations. A memoir provides a sense of time and place. Two sentences in Donald Hall's *Essays Over Eighty* say a lot in twenty-one words: "Even more, I loved the slow plod back to the barn. My grandfather told story after story with affection and humor." Think what we learn about him, his grandfather, where he lived, and their relationship in those two simple sentences! I began an essay, written ten years ago, titled "The Death of My Father, Some Forty Years On": "Sitting at the dining room table is where I remember him best. In my mind's eye my brother, Frank, is there; we are between the ages of ten and fourteen. Dishes have been cleared. One of us is sitting atop the woodstove, which heated the dining and living rooms, the warmest spot on cold winter days. It is our conversations that stay with me." (The essay can be found in my memoir, *One Man's Family*.)

Memoirs are a window into a life—a collection of anecdotes about people, events, ideas, and reflections. Aggregated, they allow the reader to learn something of the author. In a recent article in *The Wall Street Journal*, Barton Swaim wrote of the late Supreme Court justice Antonin Scalia: "A memoirist needs to interrupt his chronicle with topical discussions or reflective diversions." I thought of that sentiment, when I read in the *Financial Times* what Lucy Scholes wrote about the interplay between life and literature—a genre Joyce Carol Oates called "bibliomemoirs." Ms. Oates refers to such books as "a sub-species of literature, combining criticism and biography, with the intimate confessional tone of autobiography." But biographies based on books written are not memoirs, though books we have read say a lot about us. I have written essays about books— those I enjoyed, those I learned from, and those I collected. Write of a character that reminded you of someone you knew. Write of the books you loved as a child, of those which you kept as a reminder of long-ago days. Write of the look, smell, and feel of books on your shelves. A sketch is as valuable as a mural.

There is a temptation to fictionalize our lives. Our minds are molded to remember pleasurable moments and to erase bad ones. But we do a disservice to ourselves if we leave out the challenges we encountered, the mistakes we made, and the losses we suffered. A memoir should be honest. Memories play tricks. We sometimes claim to remember events and people we could not have known, or we remember things differently as we age. It was with humor that Gore Vidal titled his memoir *Palimpsest*. He wrote that a memoir "is not history. It is how we remember one's own life." The comedian Will Rogers once wrote, half-jokingly: "When you put down the good things you ought to have done and leave out the bad things you did well, that's memoirs." No, it isn't. Memoirs are reminders of the difference between egoism and egotism – the first, a preoccupation with one's self; the second, a narcissistic sense of conceit. A memoir demands the first but shuns the second.

E. B. White had sound advice. He once wrote: "I discovered a long time ago that writing of the small things of the day, the trivial matters of the hearth, the inconsequential but near things of this living, was the only kind of creative work which I could accomplish with any sanctity or grace." Writers must focus on details. Writing is both creative and mechanical. In terms of the latter, focus on spelling, grammar, and syntax. Use Anglo-Saxon verbs, whose definitions are never in doubt. Be merciless with adjectives and adverbs. Use short words, sentences, and paragraphs. Winston Churchill once wrote that writers should get straight to the point and aim for readers at the primary school level. Rewriting is as critical as writing. Does the essay say what you want it to say? Will the reader be certain as to your meaning? Look for the errant comma, the misplaced word, or the statement that has not been verified. Avoid repeating words. How many words, sentences, or paragraphs can be eliminated, because they detract from the point being made?

For whom are memoirs written? Unless one is famous, they are written for us, our children, and grandchildren, and for those who love history. They aid in self-understanding. They provide descendants a glimpse of their heritage. And they help us understand that, while venues, speech, and dress change, human nature remains constant over time.

Memoirs provide a worm's eye view of mankind that slides across time on a never-ending conveyor belt. We are part of that history. In that long history, our lives represent but a speck. We ride the belt for a brief period and then fall off—sad but true. But each life has meaning. It is a link, between generations, the past we know and a future we won't. Yet, we know life goes on. In my book, *Notes from Old Lyme*, in an essay titled "Another Birthday," I wrote, "I . . . look out at the snow accumulating in the fields, sense the cold of the ground underneath, but derive comfort from the knowledge that beneath that frozen soil lives the promise of spring and the resurrection of life." It is why we write. Consider how different ages think of the present. To people my age, the present is the future; to my children, the present is the present. But, to my grandchildren, the present is the past. For readers, memoirs enliven that past . . . for authors, they allow us to be the child we once were.

Stuck in a Reading Rut?
March 3, 2018

Wherever I am, if I've got that book with me, I've got a place I can go and be happy.

J. K. Rowling (1965–)
Interview with *Scholastic*, February 3, 2000, on the *Harry Potter* series

As in most things, we tend to stick to what's familiar in books we read. If one likes mysteries, and has just finished a novel by Agatha Christie, Josephine Tey, or Patricia Cornwall, one will turn to Marilyn Stasio of *The New York Times* or Otto Penzler of the Mysterious Book Shop in Manhattan to find out what they are recommending.

But does it not make sense to try something different? Recently, Erin Geiger Smith of *The Wall Street Journal* wrote an article with the title I borrowed for this piece. Her column made me think of a change I had made. I have long alternated between fiction and nonfiction. I read nonfiction to learn—history and biographies—books like Ron Chernow's *Alexander Hamilton*, David Brooks's *On Paradise Drive*, Jennet Conant's *Tuxedo Park*, and Niall Ferguson's *The Ascent of Money*. Fiction, in contrast, I used to read only for pleasure—like watching a light movie after a docudrama. I read anything by Wodehouse and everything by my daughter-in-law, Beatriz Williams. I read Robert Barnard, John Marquand, and Old Lyme's David Handler. Generally, I read about thirty books a year—not much when one considers that more than 100,000 books get published every year, but enough to keep me occupied.

But a few years ago, I decided I should read (or reread) some of the classics—Dickens, Austen, the Brontë sisters, George Eliot, even Tolkien. Reading these authors is not only entertaining, but instructional. While language and manners change, human nature does not. The exercise led me to Anthony Trollope. My parents had owned a set of Trollope, but I never read him. He seemed intimidating. However, in 2011 I picked up *Barchester Towers*. I enjoyed it but found the characters difficult to track. For five years, Trollope lay fallow. Finally, in 2016, I read *The Warden*, the first of the six Barsetshire novels. I was hooked. That same year I read *Doctor Thorne*. The characters became old friends. Last year I read *Framley Parsonage* and *The Small House at Allington*. I am

now reading *The Last Chronicle of Barset*, the final of the six books in the series, and am looking forward to starting the Parliamentary (or Palliser) series.

There are thousands of writers, and it is fun to try someone different, especially authors we read when in school or college—classics that have stood the test of time. I still like to read those I know. With the wind blowing and the rain coming down, old favorites like Charles McCarry and Lee Childs are as comfortable as a hot cup of cocoa. But we cannot spend our lives in a cocoon. No matter our age, we should challenge ourselves, and there is little that is more rewarding than rereading a book we read sixty or seventy years ago. Now, with time (and no one looking over my shoulder), I have the advantage of reading with a perspective unavailable to those in their teens.

Oh, and this essay should be shown to children and grandchildren who feel STEM programs alone lead to success. Remember, classics open the mind in a way an algebra text does not.

My library shelves

The Pleasure of Children's Books
April 25, 2020

A book, too, can be a star, 'explosive material, capable of stirring up fresh life end-
lessly,' a living fire to lighten the darkness, leading out into the expanding universe.

Madeleine L'Engle (1918–2007)
In her speech, "The Expanding Universe," August 1963

In our (relatively) new digs at Essex Meadows, shelf space is limited. About seven hundred books make their home in our apartment's library, a small fraction of what lined the walls of our much larger library in Old Lyme. Nonetheless, a number of children's favorites made the trip. They are comfortable reminders of a past that goes back eighty years. This essay speaks to five somewhat obscure children's books, four of which date to my childhood. All can be appreciated by adults.

In his essay, "On Three Kinds of Social Intercourse," Michel de Montaigne (1533–1592) wrote of slipping off to his library: "There I can turn over the leaves of this book or that, a bit of time without order or design. Sometimes my mind wanders off, at others I walk to and fro, noting down or dictating these whims of mine." Lying in bed just before falling asleep, when time knows no borders, my own youth sometimes returns in kalei-doscopic fashion—images appear, disappear, and reappear. Before nodding off, I think of books I knew and loved as a child, of years long gone.

Wolf Story, in the 1947 edition by William McCleery, sits between David McCord's 1927 essays, *Oddly Enough*, and a signed edition of Hor-ace Mann's *Inaugural Address* at Antioch College in 1854. Mr. McCleery was born in Nebraska and, as a playwright, moved to New York. In 1947 he was offered a Fellowship at the MacDowell Colony in Peter-borough, New Hampshire, which is where he wrote *Wolf Story*. The book was written for his son Michael who had accompanied his mother on her trip to Reno for a "quickie divorce." It tells the story of fic-tional five-year-old Michael who is put to bed every evening by his father, who must tell him a story— "a new story," Michael demands. The story is about a wolf named "Waldo," "the fiercest wolf in all the world," and a hen, "Rainbow," named for her colorful feathers. Michael confused the feathers of a rooster with those of a hen, which his father

A few children's books from my collection

explained but which Michael ignored. The story includes a treasured line: Michael is told to brush his teeth and wash his face before getting into bed: "Then he took a damp washcloth and gently touched his face with it, being careful not to disturb the dirt inside his ears." Every time I shower, I think of those words and smile.

When my mother died in 1990 and the house in Peterborough was emptied, a favorite book from my growing-up years ended up in our house in Greenwich. It subsequently moved up the shoreline to Old Lyme and more recently to Essex. *An Island Story: A History of England for Boys and Girls* was originally written in 1905 by H. E. Marshall. My copy sits between two newer books: *A Glorious Disaster*, by J. William Middendorf, written in 2006, which tells the story of Barry Goldwater's 1964 presidential campaign, and Frank Bruni's 2015 book on the college admissions process, *Where You Go Is Not Who You'll Be*. My copy of *An Island Story* is the first American edition, published in 1920 and in which "An" was substituted for "Our" in the title. Henrietta Elizabeth Marshall was born in Scotland in 1867 and died two weeks before I was born, in January 1941. The fact that the book was considered inaccurate from an historical perspective never troubled Ms. Marshall, or me. In the introduction she wrote: "There are many facts in school histories that seem to children to belong to lessons only. Some of those you will not find here. But you will find stories that are not to be found in your schoolbooks—stories which wise people say are only fairy stories and not history. But it seems to me that they are part of Our Island Story and should not be forgotten. . . ." The book begins with Neptune's son Albion being given an island at the request of a mermaid: "It's a beautiful little island. It lies like a gem in the bluest of waters." The story ends, in the American edition, as the Great War (World War I) came to a close and with the founding of the League of Nations. Reflecting a hope that the Great War had made the world safe for democracy, Ms. Marshall concludes with, sadly unprophetic, words from Isaiah: "The nations shall beat their swords into plowshares and their spears into pruning hooks. Nation shall not lift up a sword against nation, neither shall they learn war anymore, and none shall make them afraid." The story covers King Arthur and his Knights of the Round Table; Canute and his attempt to hold back the tide; Edward V, the king who was never crowned; Richard III and the princes in the Tower; the long reign of Victoria and the short one of her son, Edward VII. All eight of my siblings read Ms. Marshall's book. They devoured it, almost literally, as my copy had pages torn out, and reinserted in the wrong order. The book was put back together and rebound by master bookbinder Shui-min Block (wife of retired rare book dealer and friend, David Block). Shui-min also saved the watercolor illustrations by A. S. (Archibald Stevenson) Forrest (1869–1963).

Barnaby was a cartoon character, begun as a comic strip in 1942. The strip was printed in *PM*, a liberal-leaning New York newspaper that refused to accept advertising. *PM* was a weekly, published by Ralph Ingersoll and financed by Marshall Field III, and operated briefly between 1940 and 1948. The comic strip later ran in the *New York Journal-American*, until 1952. Barnaby was a cherubic, five-year-old boy who was visited by his short, cigar-smoking, four-winged fairy godfather, Jackeen J. O'Malley. He was created by children's author Crockett Johnson, also known for the 1955 book, *Harold and the Purple Crayon.* Barnaby's fairy godfather arrives one night, flying in through an open window, answering Barnaby's wish to his mother for a fairy godfather: "Cushlamochree! Broke my magic wand!" [in reality, his cigar] "You wished for a Godparent who could grant wishes? Yes, my boy, your troubles are over. O'Malley is on the job." Barnaby and his godfather got into and out of a number of scrapes. In 1943, Henry Holt and Company published Mr. Johnson's comic strip in book form, titled *Barnaby*. I had long forgotten Barnaby when, about thirty-five years ago, I saw a copy in Avenue Victor Hugo Books, a seller of used books in Lee, New Hampshire. On my shelves, *Barnaby* snuggles between a 1952 edition of Anne Frank's *Diary of a Young Girl* and the 1886 copy of *Little Lord Fauntleroy* by Frances Hodgson Burnett.

Another book from my youth was a childhood favorite of my mother's: *The Adventures of Miltiades Peterkin Paul: A Very Great Traveler Though He was Small*. In my copy, no author is listed, though it does cite John Goss and L. Hopkins as illustrators. It was published in 1916 by Lothrop, Lee, Shephard & Co., Boston. The book was in fact written by John Brownjohn, a pseudonym for Charles Remington Talbot (1851–1891) and originally published circa 1877. Talbot was an author of children's stories, often in verse. The reader is not given much detail as to when and where Miltiades was born, only that it was New England and that he was the fourth child of a farmer named Gray. While missing annual birthdays, Miltiades takes comfort in the fact he was born on February 29, because, as he says, if there had been no Leap Year that year "I suppose I should never have been born at all." His mean older brother John Henry Jack tells him that the day he was born "the sun darkened." Like Cervantes' Don Quixote, Miltiades goes forth on adventures, many of which occur as he sits, eyelids closed, in his father's library "with his feet higher than his head." He dreams, reminiscent of Alice, and his adventures begin. We learn that his great-grandfather Deuteronomy Gray was "sitting in the same position more than a hundred years before, on the morning that young Israel Putnam came down the road with his old flint-lock rifle on his shoulder and called out for him to come over to Pomfret with him." It was not the Revolution, but a wolf that had raised the alarm, inspiring Miltiades toward a new adventure. My copy, like *An Island Story*, had to be rebound, and was then boxed by Shui-min Block. *Miltiades Peterkin Paul* now sits between *The Headmaster's Papers* (1983) by Richard A. Hawley and a boxed presentation copy of *Life and Death in Shanghai* by Nien Cheng, written in 1986.

A book picked up later that had no connection to my childhood, but which makes for delicious book burrowing is a short one with cardboard covers by T. Put, published in 1905. The title: *A Catalog of Doggerel or Jokes That Was*. It is eleven pages long, illustrated, and includes this short poem:

> *The scientific students see*
> *All bent on Zo-ol (O, gee!).*
> *Say, are they here from interest,*
> *Or did they come in to rest?*
> *[If for true knowledge they would look,*
> *They ought to read this little book.]*

How could a lover of books resist? I have been unable to find anything about Mr. T. Put or the publisher, A. M. Coit. There is no library of Congress number, suggesting it may have been privately printed. Its dedication reads: "To His Birdship the Record Owl," which offers no clues, but provides a smile. The book, now encased in a handsome box, sits happily on a shelf between an 1834 edition of *Miriam Coffin* by Joseph Hart and an 1888 copy of *Sara Crewe or What Happened at Miss Minchin's*, another book by Frances Hodgson Burnett. The latter was a discard from the Middle Haddam Public Library; their waste became my treasure.

Childhood is a magical time. Despite instant communication and social networking, it still is for those born today. Cassandras should not make one believe otherwise. In childhood, everything is new. In our time, we experimented, and we learned. I envied birds in their flight, the freedom they had, disappointed that my hands and arms weren't feathered. I wanted to look down from a hundred feet—not for perspective but to spy on my sisters. Books of our childhood, such as the ones mentioned here, keep us grounded, not in the realities of science and data, but in the precious moments and magic of childhood that helped make us who we became. In *Matilda*, Roald Dahl wrote about his heroine: "The books transported her into new worlds and introduced her to amazing people who lived exciting lives."

Children's books conjure memories. They remind us of our families, that we descend from long lines of those who came before, that we are part of a continuum. They make us think of the awesome responsibility we have to future generations, to maintain hope and avoid the cynicism of a technological age. As we age and our runway shrinks, we know we must do for our grandchildren what our parents and grandparents did for us. Let them be children, encourage their reading and their imaginations. Childhood lasts only a few years. Let them be good ones. There will be time enough to be an adult. William McCleery, Henrietta Marshall, Crockett Johnson, John Brownjohn, T. Put, and a host of other authors of children's stories are allies in this process.

Fiction's Relevance
March 21, 2012

Fiction was invented the day Jonah arrived home and told his wife he was three days late because he had been swallowed by a whale.

Gabriel García Márquez (1927–2014)

Novels have long been lauded as forms of entertainment that activate the brain, provide insight into character, and present a version of events we know to be fictional yet are based on human emotions we know to be real. While there are variations, there are a finite number of human emotions, most any of which can be found described somewhere in Shakespeare or Dickens. From the website professional-counseling.com, I came across a list of 143 emotions, ranging from tense and enraged to calm and foolish. Fiction improves our understanding of people.

But novels do more. "Fiction reveals truth that reality obscures," said author Jessamyn West. Anne Murphy Paul, writing in Saturday's edition of *The New York Times*, in a piece entitled "Your Brain on Fiction," tells of studies from the field of neuroscience. The studies suggest that brain cortexes, such as olfactory, sensory, and motor, respond to reading about an experience in the same manner they do when encountering that same actuality in real life. Reading about pizza, for example, stimulates one's olfactory cortex in the same manner as walking into a pizzeria. "When subjects," Ms. Paul writes, "read a metaphor involving texture, the sensory cortex, which is responsible for perceiving texture through touch, become active." Studies by two Canadian scientists demonstrated that individuals who read fiction are better able to understand people; they empathize with them more clearly than those who do not. Some of this is self-evident, as writers often refer to fictional figures as epitomizing certain characteristics, whether they be Stuart Little, the Duke of Omnium, Oliver Twist, Elizabeth Bennet, or Hamlet.

In a world that has become increasingly digitized, it is comforting to know that scientists affirm that writers of fiction continue to perform duties for which computers are inadequate—helping to understand the complexities of society, and the interrelationships of its members. It is interesting that, like Mark Twain's premature obituary ("reports of my death are greatly exaggerated!"), the death knell for publishing has been exaggerated. Julie Bosman, writing last summer in *The New York Times*, noted that publishers in 2010 sold 2.57 billion books, in all formats, an increase of 4.1 percent over 2008, and which generated a 5.6 percent increase in revenues to $27.9 billion, during the same period. The growth in books sold was led by e-books, which increased from 0.6% of the trade market in 2008 to 6.4 percent in 2010, along with juvenile and adult fiction. One can rest assured that that rate of gain (or a faster one) for e-books will persist.

There are people who never read anything but fiction. Nevertheless, it has always seemed to me that the addition of some history and biography helps broaden the mind. However, much of history written today has the purpose of furthering a particular political agenda. Other than indisputable facts, one has to be wary that what one reads might be fiction masquerading as fact. With history and biography, it is not easy to differentiate fact from fiction. Parson Weems, in 1800 in his *Life of Washington*, used the story of Washington and the cherry tree as a metaphor to describe Washington's honesty. In reading nonfiction, skepticism is always a worthwhile antidote.

Writers of fiction may also have agendas—consider Ayn Rand and John Grisham—but the reader knows that the story is fictional. The purpose is to entertain, providing the author's insight into a complex and ever-changing world and the people who inhabit it. Since human nature does not change, classical stories—those that have withstood the test of time and were written before the advent of movies and television, when words alone were all that the author had to describe characters and emotions—have a special place in helping us understand the human condition. Fagin is unforgettable, as is Ahab, Lady Macbeth, and Undine Spragg. The reader needs no camera to recognize what the character looks like or how they will behave.

Is fiction relevant to today's world? Certainly, even in this day of IMs, tweets, texting, and Facebook; and especially so if one believes in the importance of behavior in trying to understand what moves markets or influences political leaders. All of this is a reminder to me, as on May 10 my daughter-in-law Beatriz Williams' first novel, *Overseas*, will be published, with its two memorable characters, Kate Wilson and Julian Ashford.

Imagination
December 6, 2020

But real life is only one kind of life—there is also the life of the imagination.

E. B. White (1899–1985)
Letter from E. B. White to readers of *Charlotte's Web*, 1952

Within each of us there lies a bit of James Thurber's Walter Mitty. One does not have to be a milquetoast with a demanding spouse to lapse into daydreams, to imagine impossible deeds. It is the creative urge in each of us to reach for something higher, bolder.

In *Through the Looking Glass*, Lewis Carroll had Alice, laughing, say to the White Queen: ". . . one can't believe in impossible things." The Queen replies: "I daresay you haven't had much practice. When I was younger, I always did it for half an hour a day. Why, sometimes I've believed as many as six impossible things before breakfast." Many of yesterday's impossible dreams are today's realities, thanks to creative and inventive minds.

Watch children when they play alone or with a friend. They make up characters, have them speak, and they act out fantasies. It is a learning process that breeds creativity. When my siblings and I were children, besides believing in Santa Claus, my mother told us—and we had no reason to disbelieve her—that the barn animals would converse in English at midnight on Christmas Eve. We never were able to stay awake long enough to discover if she was right, but I have no reason today to believe she fibbed. In *The Horse and His Boy*, C. S. Lewis wrote: "Shasta stroked its smooth-as-silk nose and said, 'I wish you could talk, old fellow.' And then for a second he thought he was dreaming, for quite distinctly, though in a low voice, the Horse said, 'But I can.'" And a friendship was born. In *Through the Looking Glass*, Alice finds herself in the "Garden of Live Flowers": "'O Tiger-lily,' said Alice, addressing herself to one that was waving gracefully about in the wind, 'I wish you could talk.' 'We can talk,' said the Tiger-lily, 'when there is anybody worth talking to.'" Alice passed the test. Children's imagination has been abetted by authors like Beatrix Potter, Thornton W. Burgess, Kenneth Grahame, and E. B. White, who all anthropomorphized the animals they created. None of us should grow so old or so cynical as not to be touched by Peter Rabbit, Paddy the Beaver, Mr. Toad, or Stuart Little.

Writers of fiction, like my daughter-in-law, Beatriz Williams, have great doses of imagination that allow them to create believable characters and situations. Their imagination keeps us on edge as their stories unravel. A few go to greater lengths. J. R. R. Tolkien, C. S. Lewis, and J. K. Rowling created whole worlds for their characters—Middle-earth, Narnia, and the Hogwarts School of Witchcraft and Wizardry. Miltiades Peterkin Paul, lived in his own world, where he performed deeds that finally won him his spurs . . . and a kiss from his sister Abiathar Ann.

Imagination extends beyond the literary. When I was growing up on a rocky farm in New Hampshire, I often imagined myself as someone I was not. As this was in the immediate aftermath of the Second World War, I might be the hero of a US Army raiding party against the Nazis, assaulting a pillbox filled with Japanese soldiers, or a pilot flying through shrapnel to my target in Hamburg. Or, since we had horses and political correctness was not yet discovered, my brother and I would saddle up and hunt Indians or rustlers. We did that, even though we rode "English." On other occasions, I envied birds, free of gravity's pull, flying high above, with a vista visible to me only in my imagination. A call to supper or a reminder of chores awakened us to reality. In Greenwich, while nodding off on a homeward-bound commuter train, I would imagine I was riding alone in my own private rail carriage, awakening, of course, when someone elbowed me in the ribs. Years later, sculling the marsh rivers of Old Lyme, where all signs of civilization were obscured by the aggressive (and non-native) phragmite, I would imagine myself a seventeenth-century explorer, the first to penetrate these waters and this land, until the sound of the Acela crossing the Connecticut River brought me out of my reverie. Even today, when returning to our apartment from the mailroom, I walk home along two corridors, imagining this building to be ours, each doorway an apartment where friends have been invited to stay.

It is imagination that led to great works of music and art. Think of Beethoven's Symphony no. 9, Handel's *Messiah*, Leonardo da Vinci's *The Last Supper*, and Picasso's *Guernica*. Michelangelo once said: "I saw the angel in the marble and carved until I set him free." Imagination, as well, can be sobering. Oscar Wilde, in the 1891 essay "The Critic as Artist," wrote: "Yes: I am a dreamer. For a dreamer is one who can only find his way by moonlight, and his punishment is that he sees the dawn before the rest of the world." In science, it is imagination that leads to discovery.

"Imagination is more important than knowledge," wrote Albert Einstein, "Knowledge is limited. Imagination encircles the world." Video games are examples of imagination converted into commercial products, which appeal to the imaginative instincts of teenagers. Walt Disney's Imagineering Department designs and builds their theme park attractions, resorts, and games. Almost two hundred years ago, the philosopher Jean-Jacques Rousseau told us: "The world of reality has its limits; the world of imagination is boundless."

Most people are bound by the realities of life—a job, a place to live, the raising of a family, acquiring the necessities to make life bearable. Logic and reason dominate our lives. But we should not forget, as E. B. White reminded us, that there is also the life of the imagination, and it is that which fuels our creative juices. We should not hide our Walter Mitty, yearning to be released. It is the imagination that turns a dream into an accomplishment. It is a dream of a better future that drives the immigrant, that causes a student to strive a little harder for that "A," and that guides the entrepreneur in a search for a new product or service. Dream on!

SELECTED SOURCES
AND SUGGESTIONS
FOR FURTHER READING

Abbey, Edward. *Desert Solitaire*. Tucson, AZ: The University of Arizona Press, 1968.

Armour, Richard. *Going Like Sixty; A Lighthearted Look at the Later Years*. New York: McGraw-Hill, 1974.

Brooks, David. *The Second Mountain: The Quest for a Moral Life*. New York: Random House, 2019.

Buckley, Christopher. *The Judge Hunter*. New York: Simon & Schuster, 2018.

Carroll, David M. *Swampwalker's Journal: A Wetlands Year*. New York: Houghton Mifflin, 1999.

Coady, Mary Frances. *Merton & Waugh: A Monk, A Crusty Old Man, and The Seven Storey Mountain*. Brewster, MA: Paraclete Press, 2015.

Davey, John L. *Partners in God's Love*. Maitland, FL: Xulon Press, 2007.

Earle, Captain George. *History of the 87th Mountain Infantry, Italy 1945*. Boulder, CO: Bradford Robinson, 1945.

Geisel, Theodor Seuss. *How the Grinch Stole Christmas*. New York: Random House, 1957.

—. *I Can Read with My Eyes Shut*. New York: Random House, 1978.

Grotz, Jennifer. *The Needle*. New York: Houghton Mifflin Harcourt, 2011.

Hall, Donald. *Essays Over Eighty*. New York: Houghton Mifflin Harcourt, 2014.

Hitchens, Christopher. *And Yet. . . .* New York: Simon & Schuster, 2015.

Johnston, Joseph F. Jr. *The Decline of Nations: Lessons for Strengthening America at Home and in the World*. Alexandria, VA: Republic Book Publishers, 2020.

Kingsolver, Barbara. *Homeland and Other Stories*. New York: HarperCollins, 1989.

Lewis, C. S. *The Horse and His Boy*. London: Geoffrey Bles, 1954.

—. *The Lion, the Witch and the Wardrobe*. London: Geoffrey Bles, 1950.

—. *C. S. Lewis: Essay Collection and Other Short Pieces*. Edited by Lesley Walmsley. London: HarperCollins, 2000.

Lindbergh, Charles A. *The Spirit of St. Louis*. New York: Charles Scribner's Sons, 1953.

Rothschild, Hannah. *House of Trelawney*. New York: Knopf, 2020.

Scalia, Antonin. Scalia Speaks: *Reflections on Law, Faith, and Life Well Lived*. New York: Crown Forum, 2017.

Skinner, Burrhus Frederic. *Contingencies of Reinforcement: A Theoretical Analysis*. New York: Appleton-Century-Crofts, 1969.

Spiegelman, Willard. *Senior Moments: Looking Back, Looking Ahead*. New York: Farrar, Straus and Giroux, 2016.

Spollen, Anne. *The Shape of Water*. Mendota Heights, MN: Flux, 2008.

Steinbeck, John. *Travels with Charley: In Search of America*. New York: Viking, 1962.

Strunk, William Jr., and E. B. White. *The Elements of Style*. New York: Macmillan Publishing, 1959.

Teale, Edwin Way, ed. *The Wilderness World of John Muir*. New York: Houghton Mifflin, 1954.

Tolkien, J. R. R. *The Lord of the Rings: The Fellowship of the Ring*. London: Allen & Unwin, 1954.

—. *The Lord of the Rings: The Return of the King*. London: Allen & Unwin, 1955.

White, E. B. *Charlotte's Web*. New York: Harper & Brothers, 1952.

—. *Essays of E. B. White*. New York: HarperCollins Publishers, 1977.

—. *Here Is New York*. New York: Harper & Brothers, 1949.

—. *Letters of E. B. White*. Edited by Dorothy Lobrano Guth. New York: Harper & Row, 1976.

—. *Stuart Little*. New York: Harper & Brothers, 1945.

—. *The Points of My Compass: Letters from the East, the West, the North, the South*. New York: Harper & Row, 1962.

Wodehouse, P. G. *The Inimitable Jeeves*. London: Herbert Jenkins, 1923.

—. *Mr. Mulliner Speaking*. London: Herbert Jenkins, 1929.

Wohlleben, Peter. *The Inner Life of Animals*. Vancouver: Greystone Books, 2017.

—. *The Hidden Life of Trees*. Vancouver: Greystone Books, 2016.

Zinsser, William. *On Writing Well*. New York: Harper & Row, 1976.